Calendar Events

By
Jean Stangl

Cover illustration by
Margo de Paulis

Inside illustrations by
Julie Anderson

Publishers
T.S. Denison & Company, Inc.
Grand Rapids, Michigan 49504

Standard Book Number: 513-02264-3
Calendar Events
Copyright © 1995 by T.S. Denison & Co., Inc.
Grand Rapids, Michigan 49504
Printed in USA

TABLE OF CONTENTS

Introduction

Do you want to find new and fun ways for your students to celebrate days, weeks and months as well as innovative ways to celebrate regular holidays? *Calendar Events* is the book for you!

Introduce your students to ways they can learn about, as well as celebrate,
>
> National Snack Food Month
> National Adopt-A-Cat Month
> National Foot Health Month
> American Chocolate Week
> National Coin Week
> Pickled Pepper Week
> Limerick Day
> No Socks Day
> World's Largest Pizza Anniversary
> Alaska Admission Day

and over 200 other "special" months, weeks, and days.

This valuable resource book provides unusual information on holidays, anniversaries, birthdays, and special events as well as innovative ways to celebrate regular holidays. Most of the activities are short and take only a little classroom time and preparation, and can be worked into any time of the day or any areas of the curriculum.

The easy-to-follow directions for activities encourage research and introduce sources for locating information so students can make new discoveries.

Select the special days that interest you and that you feel will have special appeal to your students and write them on the blank calendar that can also be duplicated for student use.

For year-around schools and youth programs, special days and activities are included for June, July, and August. Church and religious schools will find ideas for related special events and days to celebrate.

There are over fifty reproducibles including a perpetual calendar, patterns for making related crafts and puppets, and math, history, art, and geography "fun sheets."

Calendar Events provides an excellent, one-of-a-kind resource to add fun, humor, and uniqueness to learning as well as reinforcing developing mental skills.

Part One
Calendars

In ancient times, before there were calendars, people would base the beginning of the new year on the run of salmon or the flooding of the Nile River. Marks were made on caves or walls to keep track of time.

We can see the moon change from a thin crescent to a full moon and back again every 291/2 days. Watching the moon and noting the changes is one way of keeping track of time.

The Hebrew year is based on the moon and normally consists of twelve months. Have students find out the names of these twelve months and the number of days in each.

It was not until early in this century that most countries had accepted the Gregorian calendar and everyone began celebrating the new year at the same time. Great Britain adopted the Gregorian calendar on September 14, 1752. Special new year celebrations are also based on other calendars such as the Jewish Rosh Hashanah and the Chinese New Year.

Assign students or small groups to see what they can find out about these two calendars. Other calendars such as the Julian Calendar and the Islamic Calendar would also be interesting calendars to research.

Elizabeth Achelis created a new calendar called "The World Calendar." She divided the year into four quarters. However, her system left two extra days which she named "Worldsdays." Students will be fascinated by a wealth of information on this calendar, as well as on other calendars, found in a book by Marilyn Burns called *This Book is About Time*, A Brown Paper School Book (Little Brown). If you can find the book, have a small group make a report on it.

It might seem to students that the new year should begin in September since it is back-to-school month. Divide the class into groups to present the pros and cons.

Add each new month to the current spelling list.

Try to locate the birthstone for each month, either in a piece of jewelry or a color picture of the stone. Bring in real flowers whenever possible, or use realistic plastic ones or pictures cut from seed and flower catalogs.

At the beginning of the year, check with print shops or banks for small calendars for each student to use as a reference.

Calendar Activities:

1. Areas for research: how spring, summer, fall, and winter are determined, and why we have Leap Year.

2. Use your birthday month to find out about that particular month. Based on this information, make a collage by either drawing pictures or using pictures found in magazines. Include the month's birthstone, flower, poems, or other written bits of information.

3. At the beginning of the year, have each student bring in one calendar. Compare the similarities and differences among the calendars. Ask students for input as to who would give away free calendars and why.

4. Over twenty new words can be made from the word "September." Have students see how many words they can make. "Calendar" is another word with many possibilities. Challenge students to try any or all of the other months.

5. Give each student a copy of "Name That Month" (page 7) to complete.

6. Give each student a copy of "Best Wishes" (page 8) to complete.

7. Give each student a copy of "All About Months" (page 9) to complete.

Name That Month

Write in the name of the correct month and the number of days it has.

Order	Name of the Month	Number of Days
1st	_____	_____
2nd	_____	_____
3rd	_____	_____
4th	_____	_____
5th	_____	_____
6th	_____	_____
7th	_____	_____
8th	_____	_____
9th	_____	_____
10th	_____	_____
11th	_____	_____
12th	_____	_____

Best Wishes

Fill in the blanks with your own best wishes for the year. Look carefully at the numbers. The first line is filled in for you.

1 _____year_____ of _____happiness_____

12 _____ of _____

52 _____ of _____

365 _____ of _____

8,760 _____ of _____

525,600 _____ of _____

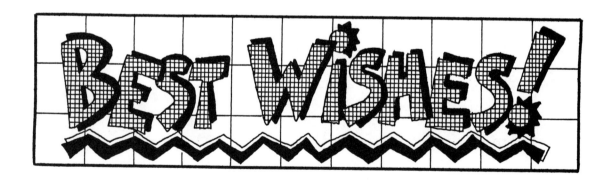

All About Months

Which are the two months that start with the letter A? _____

_____

Which are the three months that start with the letter J? _____

_____

What is the last month of the year? _____

What is the first month of the year? _____

Which month has the shortest name? _____

Which are the two middle months? _____

Which month is the seventh month? _____

Which month is the fourth month? _____

Which months end in "ber"? _____

_____

Which is the only month that changes the number of days it contains?

_____

How many months have 30 days? _____

How many months have 31 days? _____

Which month is your birthday month? _____

How many days does your birthday month have? _____

Name _____

Make Your Own Month

_____

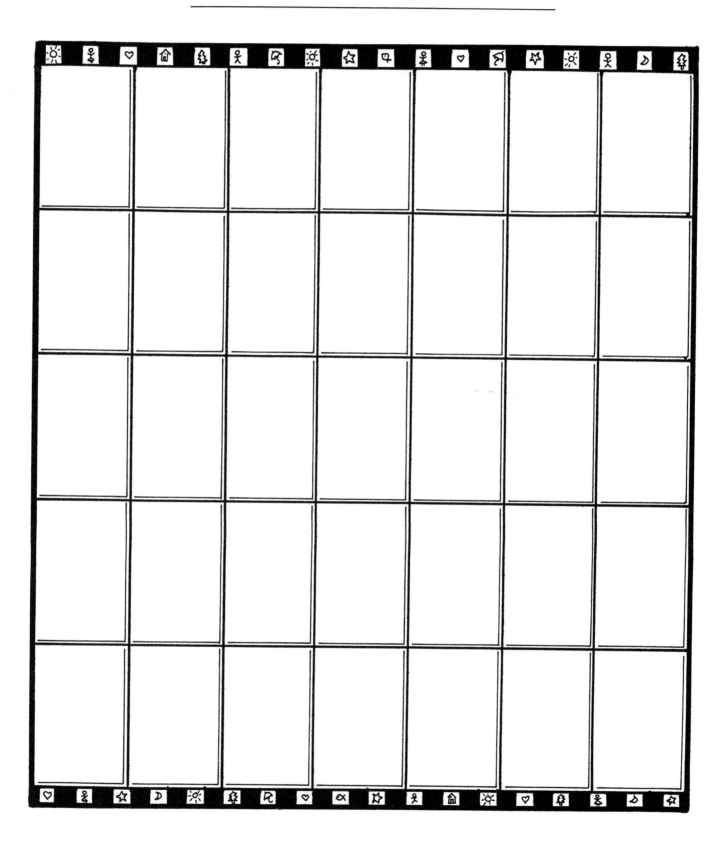

Part Two
Holidays and Special Days

A holiday is a day when people put aside regular duties and take a day off from their job or school. Sunday is the only holiday recognized by common law.

Under the listing for each month in Part Four, it may read the 2nd or 3rd week which usually means the 2nd or 3rd full week.

National or federal holidays are days on which post offices, banks, federal offices and schools are closed.

Presidential proclamations, such as the three-day weekend for President's Day and the change made for Thanksgiving Day are first introduced in the House of Representatives or the Senate. The first such proclamation was by President Washington declaring November 26, 1789 as Thanksgiving Day. Proclamations are made to commemorate people, events, ideas, and activities worthy of national recognition.

Special state holidays are declared by the governor, and local holidays, festivals and special events by the mayor. This might include Founder's Day, or the recognition of an important personality or event. This could be a special day, week or month.

Explain to students that many festivals and events are held for commercial purposes or to promote a product and are generally sponsored by an organization, company, business, or association.

Some local celebrations are Hog Calling Contest Days in Weatherford, Oklahoma, on February 17 and National Pig Day in Lubbock, Texas, on March 1.

There is Irish Heritage Week in Arkansas and Maple Syrup Day in Appleton, Wisconsin, Vermont and several other places.

March 21 is Bird Day in Iowa and there is Buzzard's Day held in Hinckley, Ohio, in March. Garlic, spinach, apples, and strawberries all have a "special day" in some states.

Activities:

1. Find out when and why the celebration of some holidays has been changed, such as Thanksgiving and President's Day, and why and when the three-day weekend celebrations came into being.

2. Find out about local celebrations in your city and nearby areas.

3. Find out if your city celebrates its founding, when it is, and how the event is celebrated.

4. Have each student create a special holiday for his or her city. Tell why it should be declared a special day (week or month) and how it would be celebrated.

Part Three
Maps

Make copies of the United States Map "A" (page 13) for younger students to use when adding the state admission date. Use "B" (page 14) for older students who can identify and write in the name of the state.

Use the Admission Order (page 15) for students to write in the order the states were admitted.

Map Activities:
1. Total the number of states admitted during each month. Use the information to make a graph. Use different squares or circles of paper to represent each state.

2. Have older students locate the capitals on a large classroom map and write them in their proper places on the map.

3. Find out how many years your state has been a state *(clue: subtract the admission date from this year's date).*

4. Give students a copy of one of the maps and crayons or felt pens. Give directions for locating and then coloring, such as color Texas green, color the largest state blue, and color all the West Coast states yellow.

5. Assign each student one or two states. On 3" x 5" cards, have each write the name of the state and the admission date. You may wish to have older students include additional information. Write the name of each month on different colored strips of paper and tape them across the top of the bulletin board. Attach a length of yarn to each month. Have students tape their states onto the yarn under the appropriate months.

6. Make a giant-sized classroom time line. Use a long roll of shelf paper and make a heavy line across the center. Start with 1787 and end with 1959. Mark on the time line the years in which states were admitted. Older students can add names of states at each time line. You may wish to have small groups work on parts of the time line and then tape the completed line together.

7. Have each student check the time line and then write down the year that the most states were admitted; a year no states were admitted; how many were admitted in 1787; the number admitted in the 1700s, the 1800s, and the 1900s.

The United States – Map A

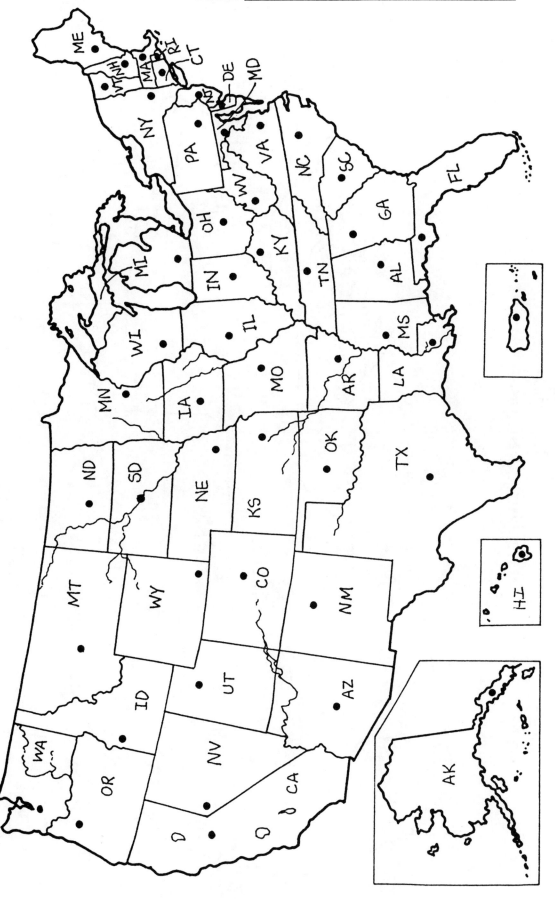

Name _____

The United States – Map B

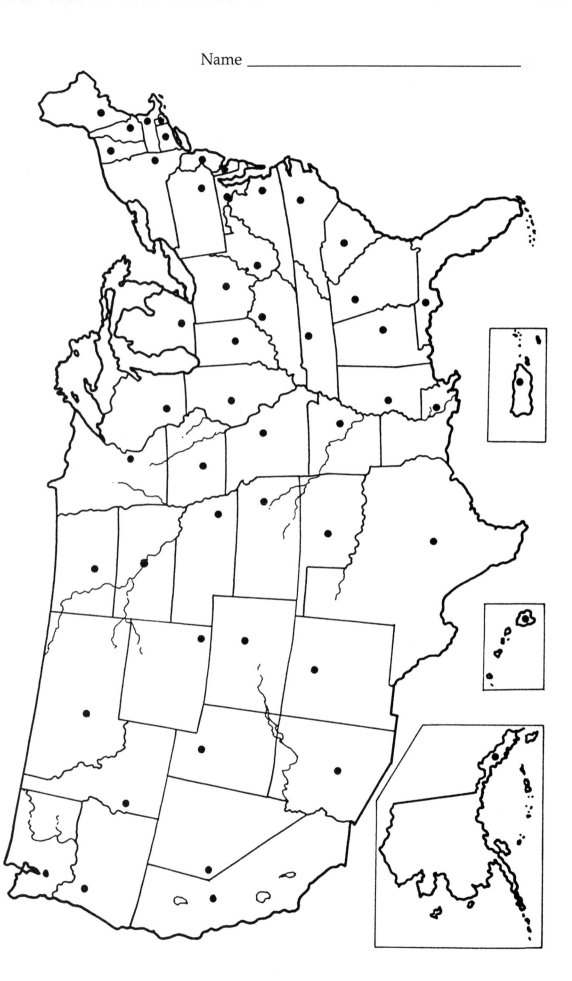

State Admission Order

1. _____
2. _____
3. _____
4. _____
5. _____
6. _____
7. _____
8. _____
9. _____
10. _____
11. _____
12. _____
13. _____
14. _____
15. _____
16. _____
17. _____
18. _____
19. _____
20. _____
21. _____
22. _____
23. _____
24. _____
25. _____

26. _____
27. _____
28. _____
29. _____
30. _____
31. _____
32. _____
33. _____
34. _____
35. _____
36. _____
37. _____
38. _____
39. _____
40. _____
41. _____
42. _____
43. _____
44. _____
45. _____
46. _____
47. _____
48. _____
49. _____
50. _____

Name _____

This is My State

Draw a picture to show each thing listed.

My state
☆ ☆ ☆ ☆

My state tree
🌲 🌲 🌲 🌲 🌲 🌲

My state animal
🐄 🐄 🐄 🐄 🐄

My state flower
🌸 🌸 🌸 🌸 🌸 🌸

My state bird
🐦 🐦 🐦 🐦

My state motto
🗨 🗨 🗨 🗨 🗨

My state flag
🚩 🚩 🚩 🚩 🚩

Our United States

Use your United States Map, the State Admission Order (page 15), and the bulletin board state cards to help you find the answers.

1. Which month had the most states admitted? _____

2. Which months had two states admitted?_____

   _____

3. Which months had only one state admitted? _____

   _____

4. How many months had six states admitted? _____

   _____

5. How many months had three states admitted? _____

   _____

6. How many months had five states admitted? _____

   _____

7. In which month was the first state admitted?_____

8. In which month was the last state admitted? _____

9. In which month was your state admitted? _____

10. How many other states were admitted in the same month as your state?

    _____

    _____

Part Four
Months of the Year
January

Flower – Snowdrop or carnation
Birthstone – Garnet

The first month, January, is named for Janus, a Roman God. It originally contained only thirty days, but Julius Caesar added a day to make thirty-one days. Some people called the month Wolfmonth. Students may speculate as to why it was called by that name, and then do research to find the answer.

In the northern half of the world, this is usually the coldest month; in the southern half, it is usually the warmest.

MONTH

NATIONAL EYE HEALTH CARE MONTH
Celebrate by:
1. Have each student use a pencil to punch a hole through the center of a piece of construction paper. Have them hold the papers still, look through the holes, and then describe what they see: Viewing the same area with first one eye and then the other will help them understand that we can see more with two eyes than with one.
2. Check the encyclopedia (or other sources) for a picture of the eye and explain how the eye works.
3. Look at pictures of the eyes of insects that have compound eyes. Have students write a short fantasy story or poem about themselves and their special compound eyes.
4. Stress the importance of caring for our eyes. Invite an ophthalmologist to visit or look into having the school district or county health service come and check the students' eyes.

NATIONAL HOBBY MONTH
Celebrate by:
1. Discuss hobbies such as things one enjoys doing or collecting. Have children share their hobbies. Decide on a class (or small group) hobby or collection. Students can collect materials, find ways to display the collection, make posters, and decorate a bulletin board.
2. Invite a parent or someone from the community who has an unusual hobby, to visit and share with the class.
3. Encourage students who do not have a hobby to start one. Plan a hobby share day, or have students take turns sharing their hobbies over a several day period.

NATIONAL HOT TEA MONTH

Celebrate by:

1. Research tea-growing countries and make a graph showing the top countries that grow tea.
2. Provide an assortment of herbal teas, cups and hot water for each student to make a cup of tea. Take turns describing the taste of the tea. Save the tea leaves.
3. Dry the tea leaves. Spread liquid glue on a piece of paper. Sprinkle the dry tea leaves onto the wet glue, forming a design of the students' choice. Cover the leaves with a piece of wax paper and press to the glue. Let dry.

NATIONAL OATMEAL MONTH

Celebrate by:

1. Bring in a box of oatmeal. Have students examine a pinch of dry oatmeal by feeling and tasting it. Read the ingredients on the box.
2. Ask students from where they think oatmeal comes. Check encyclopedias or other sources to find out.
3. Have each student bring in an empty box (or a coupon or newspaper ad) from oat cereal. Set up a display. Count and record the number of different varieties students found.
4. Read the labels on the boxes to see what else the cereal contains. Compare the amount of sugar and salt found in the cereals.

NATIONAL PRUNE BREAKFAST MONTH

Celebrate by:

1. Find out if students know what a prune is, from where it comes, and how it becomes a prune.
2. Compare canned and fresh plums to dried prunes. Give each student a pitted prune to eat.
3. On a classroom chart, have students write ways prunes are served, such as stewed, stuffed with nuts or cream cheese, prune pudding and prune cake.
4. Prepare one of the selections given and serve with a sample of prune juice.

NATIONAL SOUP MONTH

Celebrate by:

1. Have students bring in labels from cans of soup during a two week period. Total the amount collected. Sort by varieties. Sort by brands.
2. Vote by ballot for their favorite soup. Tally the votes.
3. Serve the students' favorite soup.
4. Use the information from #1 and #2 to create class graphs. Try to make each a different type of graph—line, picture, solid.
5. Display the labels on the bulletin board for the remainder of the month.

1 – 7 UNIVERSAL LETTER-WRITING WEEK
Celebrate by:
1. Discuss letter-writing—legibility, date, greeting (salutation), closing, and signing. Have students write letters to friends or family members.
2. Write a letter to an imaginary pen pal.
    Names and addresses for pen pals can be found in teacher magazines and many children's magazines. For those who wish, they can write to real pen pals.
3. Older students can learn to address an envelope correctly.
4. Older students can write a business letter such as a letter to the editor of a newspaper or magazine, a complimentary letter to a business, government agency or organization.

2nd week (week that includes the 17th) INTERNATIONAL PRINTING WEEK
Celebrate by:
1. Make your own stamp pad. Fold two or three paper towels (or use a thin sponge) and place the pad in a flat pan. Pour paint onto the paper towel until it is saturated. Use tops cut from vegetables, kitchen tools (potato masher, whisk, tines on a fork), cardboard tubes and other items to stamp prints onto paper.
2. Look through newspapers and magazines and note the graphics used.
3. Arrange to visit a printing shop or a newspaper office to see how printing is handled.
4. Arrange to visit or invite to your class a student or the instructor from the graphic arts department of a college or university.
5. Check the Yellow Pages for the name of a local graphic artist and ask him or her to visit and demonstrate his or her technique.

Week that includes the 27th – MOZART WEEK
Celebrate by:
1. Divide the class into groups and assign a research project to each: research Mozart's early life; what made him famous; bring in one or more pictures of Mozart (found in music books and encyclopedias); what kinds of music Mozart composed (he composed music for the piano, harpsichord, and flute, as well as other instruments); find pictures of these three instruments.
2. Have a group share their reports, one each day for the week.
3. Mozart was born in Salzburg, Austria. Find the country and city on a classroom map.

1 NEW YEAR'S DAY
Celebrate by:
1. This date is a legal holiday in the United States and many other countries. Write an essay on how your family celebrates New Year's.
2. Assign small groups and have each group research how another country celebrates this day. Share your research and point out the country on the classroom map.
3. Discuss resolutions and goals. Resolutions are seldom kept; goals are a challenge and give us something to look forward to and work toward attaining. Give each student a copy of the "Past and Present" (page 29) face. Have them cut out their faces, then write down two positive events that happened to them in the past year on the "past" side, and two realistic short term and two long term goals for themselves on the "future" side of the faces. Keep the faces in a file and have students read over their goals on the first of every month.

1 PAUL REVERE'S BIRTHDAY
Celebrate by:
1. This American patriot was born in Boston, Massachusetts. One night he went for a ride on a borrowed horse. Assign the following research questions to each student: a) When was he born? b) When was his famous ride? c) When did he die? Make a time line to show these dates.
2. Read the poem, "Paul Revere's Ride" (page 32) by Longfellow, to the class.
3. Discuss the poem by asking the following: what was the name of the war; between what two cities did Paul Revere ride; what signal could be seen from the church tower; what did the signal signify?

1 BETSY ROSS' BIRTHDAY (1752–1836)
Celebrate by:
1. *See:* June 14, Flag Day. Betsy Ross was a seamstress who is given credit for making the first American flag from a design given to her by a committee headed by George Washington. Make copies of "The First Flag" (page 30) for students to color.
2. Compare the first flag to our flag today. Find similarities and differences.
3. Find pictures showing the changes in our flag from the first one to the present. Make a time line to show the dates of the changes. Draw small pictures of the flags at the appropriate time periods on the time line.

2 GEORGIA ADMISSION DAY
Celebrate by:
1. Georgia became the 4th state in 1788. Add this information to your United States map (page 13). Color the state lightly with colored pencil or crayon.
2. Write the state opposite its number on the State Admission Order page (page 15).

3 ALASKA ADMISSION DAY
Celebrate by:
1. Alaska became the 49th state in 1959. Add this information to your United States map (page 13). Color the state lightly with colored pencil or crayon.
2. Write the state opposite its number on the State Admission Order page (page 15).

3 JOAN WALSH ANGLUND'S BIRTHDAY (1926 –   )
Celebrate by:
1. Joan Walsh Anglund is an author and illustrator of children's books. On a visit to the library, see how many of her books you can find. Read one or more to the class.
2. Make the books available in the classroom. Encourage students to examine the illustrations. What is unusual about them? (Her illustrations of children have only eyes, no other facial features.)

3 WAXED PAPER DRINKING STRAWS PATENTED (1888)
Celebrate by:
1. Give each student a waxed paper drinking straw and a cup of water. Have them suck in on the straw; then blow out. Discuss the affect of air in this experiment. Add liquid soap to the cup of water and blow bubbles. Find out about bubbles.
2. Ask students to share other ways a straw can be used for experiments or tricks.
3. Start a class collection of straws. Find similarities and differences among the straws in the collection.

4 LOUIS BRAILLE (1809–1852)
Celebrate by:
1. Louis Braille, a Frenchman and teacher of the blind, invented the Braille alphabet. Blinded at the age of three, Louis Braille later invented an alphabet that could be "read" by touching raised dots. Older children can take turns leading a partner while blindfolded. Have students share how it felt when they could not see.
2. Ask your librarian for a book in braille that can be shown to the class. Howe Press, Perkins School of the Blind, Watertown, Massachusetts, publishes children's books, such as Robert McCloskey's *Make Way for Ducklings*, in braille.
3. Check local services for a teacher of the visually impaired as a possible visitor to your class.

4 JACOB WILHELM GRIMM'S BIRTHDAY (1785–1863)
Celebrate by:
1. Jacob and his brother wrote down a collection of fairy tales that were told orally in Germany. Ask students to bring in books of any collections they might have. Examine the books and draw attention to the illustrations in the early collections.
2. Give students a few days to examine and read through some of the collections. Read the titles of some of the fairy tales. Have students write on a slip of paper their favorite Grimm fairy tale. Collect and sort the votes.
3. Make a graph to show the favorites.
4. Read one or two of the favorites to the class.

4 UTAH ADMISSION DAY

Celebrate by:

1. Utah became the 45th state in 1896. Add this information to your United States map (page 13). Color the state lightly with crayon or colored pencil.
2. Write this state opposite its number on the State Admission Order page (page 15).

5 GEORGE WASHINGTON CARVER'S DEATH ANNIVERSARY (1943)

Celebrate by:

1. He was probably born in 1859, but the exact date is unknown. Assemble a collection of books on George Washington Carver for the students to read.
2. Carver made more than 300 products from the peanut. Start a classroom chart to record the products as students discover them through their reading.
3. Have students locate as many pictures as possible of the products listed on the chart. Add the pictures to a bulletin board along with information on Mr. Carver.

6 NEW MEXICO ADMISSION DAY

Celebrate by:

1. New Mexico became our 47th state in 1912. Add this information to your United States map (page 13). Color the state lightly with crayon or colored pencil.
2. Write this state opposite its number on the State Admission Order page (page 15).

9 CONNECTICUT ADMISSION DAY

Celebrate by:

1. Connecticut became our 5th state in 1788. Add this information to your United States map (page 13). Color the state lightly with crayon or colored pencil.
2. Write this state opposite its number on the State Admission Order page (page 15).

10 ANNIVERSARY OF THE DISCOVERY OF OIL IN TEXAS (1901)

Celebrate by:

1. Do research to find out different uses for oil.
2. Find out which other states produce oil and locate these states on the classroom map.
3. Have students first predict and then experiment to find out if oil is heavier or lighter than water. Do this by pouring equal amounts of water and cooking oil into a flat pan. Observe and discuss what takes place.

12 CHARLES PERRAULT'S BIRTHDAY (1628–1703)

Celebrate by:

1. Who was Charles Perrault? (He was a French author who wrote fairy tales such as *Cinderella*, *Puss In Boots*, and *Little Red Riding Hood*.) Locate some of his works. Read them aloud.
2. Compare Perrault's fairy tales to those of the Grimm brothers.

15 MARTIN LUTHER KING JR.'S BIRTHDAY (1929–1968)
Celebrate by:
1. "I have a dream" are famous words from Dr. Martin Luther King, Jr., who was a leader in the struggle for equal rights for African American citizens. What was his dream?
2. Draw a picture that shows Dr. King's dream coming true.
3. Have each student trace around his or her open hand. Cut out and glue yarn around the edges of the hands. Attach to the bulletin board in a large circle (to represent the world). Link the hands together with a length of yarn.

16 NATIONAL NOTHING DAY
Celebrate by:
1. Take turns sharing why students think National Nothing Day should be a national holiday.
2. Write down two ways to celebrate National Nothing Day.
3. Set a timer and instruct students to sit and do "nothing" for one minute; then for two minutes; then three minutes. At the end of the time, ask them if they still feel we should have a "do nothing" holiday.
   This special day was created in 1973 by a newspaperman named Harold Pullman Coffin. It was originally meant to be a day people could sit without observing, honoring, or celebrating anything. But did we not just discover that it is not any fun doing nothing?

17 BENJAMIN FRANKLIN'S BIRTHDAY (1706–1790)
Celebrate by:
1. Assign to small groups topics on Benjamin Franklin to research and present to the class: childhood, inventor/scientist, publisher/author, public servant, statesman.
2. Read and discuss the book, *Ben and Me* by Robert Lawson (Viking) – a biography of Ben Franklin from a mouse's point of view.
3. Benjamin Franklin used rebuses in a short tract called, "The Art of Making Money Plenty." A rebus is a word game in which numbers, letters and pictures are used to indicate names, words and phrases such as I ♥ U. Read rebus stories or puzzles from a children's magazine. Older children can create a short rebus.

17 QUEEN LILIUOKALINA LOST HER THRONE (1893)
Celebrate by:
1. Queen Liliuokalina was the only reigning queen to live and rule in Iolani Palace (America's only recognized palace) in Honolulu, Hawaii. Find out how she became queen and why she lost her throne. Only one king ever lived in the palace—who was he?
2. There are only twelve letters in the Hawaiian alphabet. The queen's name contains seven of those letters. List them on a classroom chart and challenge the students to find out the remaining five (a e h i k l m n o p u w). Every Hawaiian word and syllable ends in a vowel. See if students know any words in the Hawaiian language. *Examples:* hale=house; ae=yes; ai=eat; aole=no; hula=dance; pua=flower; wikiwiki= to hurry.
3. Make leis by stringing paper or plastic flowers (or cut apart colored egg carton cups) on a length of yarn.
4. Invite someone of Hawaiian background to teach the hula to the students.

17 SHARI LEWIS' BIRTHDAY (1934 -)
Celebrate by:
1. Shari Lewis is a puppeteer who was born in New York City. She is known for her puppets which were made famous by her television programs. How old is she? Do you know the names of any of her puppets? Have students check with parents, older friends or relatives.
2. Discuss the differences between puppets and marionettes.
3. Make copies of the hand puppet (page 31) for students. Trace and cut the puppet from cloth or heavy paper. Sew or staple the edges and decorate.

18 PAUL REVERE'S RIDE ANNIVERSARY (1775)
Celebrate by:
1. Make copies of "Paul Revere's Ride" (page 32) for each student. Have them take turns, each reading lines of the poem. Repeat as needed or you may wish to locate a copy of the entire poem for reading.
2. Illustrate the poem in a medium of your choice.
3. Read the poem to the class, pausing when appropriate, and have students mime the action.

18 POOH DAY
Celebrate by:
1. This day is in honor of Winnie the Pooh's creator, A.A. Milne's (Alan Alexander), birthday (1882–1956). What are the names of some of Winnie the Pooh's story book friends?
2. Read some of Milne's stories and poetry.
3. Check with students and parents to see if anyone has copies of first edition books, recordings, or other memorabilia they can share.
4. *Pooh Cookbook* by Virginia Ellison (Dell, 1975) contains reading selections and easy-to-make recipes.

18 PETER MARK ROGET'S BIRTHDAY (1779–1843)
Celebrate by:
1. Who was this man? Roget was an English physician and the author of *Roget's Thesaurus*. What is a thesaurus? The word means treasury and the first thesaurus was published in 1852.
2. Provide thesauruses for students to examine, and show them how to use the book. Give each student a word to investigate.
3. A thesaurus is also a dictionary and introduces antonyms and synonyms. Explain the two terms and refer to examples.
4. Roget also invented the "log, log" slide rule. What is a slide rule and what is its use? If possible, share one or more with the class and demonstrate how to use it. Try a few addition and subtraction problems. Ask why they think a slide rule is outdated.

20 NATIONAL HAT DAY
Celebrate by:
1. Provide paper bags, paper plates, newspapers and decorating materials for kids to create their own hats. Provide several hand mirrors.
2. Have a hat parade by parading around the play yard, through the cafeteria, or into other classrooms (seek permission if needed).
3. Invite personnel from the office, the principal, custodian and others to come to your class to view a hat exhibit. Invite them to make their own hats. Students can help them with their creations.

23 JOHN HANCOCK'S BIRTHDAY (1737–1793)

Celebrate by:

1. Instruct students to take a piece of paper and in the upper right-hand corner put their "John Hancock." Ask for input as to what the term means and how it originated (John Hancock was the first signer of the Declaration of Independence).
2. Read and discuss the Preamble to the Declaration of Independence.

23 NATIONAL HANDWRITING DAY

Celebrate by:

1. Assign students a sentence to write. Have them practice and then copy in the best hand writing they can. Collect and pin to the bulletin board (no names on the handwriting samples but number each one).
2. Have small groups take turns going to the bulletin board and writing down the number and the student's name whose handwriting they think it is.
3. Have each student practice his or her name by printing, cursive, and calligraphy—the art of fine handwriting. Ask a parent or friend to come and give a demonstration of calligraphy.
4. Research the history of handwriting. Check with parents or others in the community who may know of someone who can demonstrate Chinese or Japanese handwriting.

23 NATIONAL PIE DAY

Celebrate by:

1. On a classroom chart, list the students' favorite pies. Use the information to make a graph. Colored circles can be used to represent each vote for a particular choice.
2. Have students bring in a recipe for "the most unusual pie contest" (include meat and vegetable pies).
3. Make individual pies in foil cupcake papers. Make a graham cracker crust and fill with instant pudding. Follow the directions on the boxes.

26 MICHIGAN ADMISSION DAY

Celebrate by:

1. Michigan became our 26th state in 1837. Add this information to your United States map (page 13). Lightly color the state with crayons or colored pencils.
2. Write this state opposite its number on the State Admission Order page (page 15).

27 CHARLES LUTWIDGE DODGSON'S BIRTHDAY (1832–1898)

Celebrate by:

1. Who was he? (He was Lewis Carroll, a mathematics teacher and author of the Alice books.) Read portions from some of his books.
2. Write a story from a white rabbit's point of view about falling through a chimney of a castle.

27 WOLFGANG AMADEUS MOZART'S BIRTHDAY (1756–1791)

Celebrate by:

1. Mozart began composing music at the age of five. He was born in Salzburg, Austria. Locate the city on a map. Play a recording of one of Mozart's piano compositions, and then play a recording by a contemporary artist. Compare the two pieces.
2. Invite a parent or local pianist to come and play some of Mozart's work.
3. Have students read about Mozart from an encyclopedia, biography, or other resources. Write a four-line poem, a limerick, or a riddle about Mozart.

Fourth Wednesday NATIONAL SCHOOL NURSE DAY

Celebrate by:

1. Have students make thank-you cards for the school nurse. Younger children can draw pictures.
2. Create a song about your school nurse to the tune of a familiar song.
3. Invite the school nurse to come to class and talk about his or her job. Then surprise him or her with the cards, pictures and song.

27 KANSAS ADMISSION DAY

Celebrate by:

1. Kansas became our 34th state in 1861. Add this information to your United States map (page 13). Lightly color the state with crayon or colored pencil.
2. Write this state opposite its number on the State Admission Order page (page 15).

28 GREAT SEAL OF THE UNITED STATES ANNIVERSARY

Celebrate by:

1. Congress first recognized the need for a seal of the United States on this date in 1782. Locate a picture of the seal. Find out what it represents and how and where it is used.
2. Locate a picture of your state seal and compare the two seals.

29 ICE CREAM CONE ROLLING MACHINE PATENTED (1924)

Celebrate by:

1. Roll a piece of butcher paper to form a cone. Tape the edges. Before the machine was invented, cones were rolled by hand. Discuss why this would not be practical today.
2. Save the cone to fill with popcorn on National Popcorn Day, January 31.
3. Name other things that are cone-shaped.

31 NATIONAL POPCORN DAY

Celebrate by:

1. *See:* October, National Popcorn Poppin' Month. What makes popcorn pop? Examine popcorn before and after popping and compare the two forms.
2. In three empty film canisters, place 5, 10, and 15 kernels of corn. Seal the lids and mark them: ?, !, #. Have students write down the symbols, and after shaking each canister, write the estimated number of kernels after the symbols.
3. Measure enough popcorn to make a popper of corn. Have students estimate the number of unpopped kernels that will be in the popper after the corn is popped. Make popcorn and serve in the cones you saved from January 29. Count the number of unpopped kernels and compare to the estimates.

31 MOON LANDING WITH HAM THE CHIMPANZEE
Celebrate by:
1. Apollo 14 was launched on this date in 1971. Who were the two men who landed on the moon? (Alan Shepard and Edgar Mitchell).
2. Have students write a story about themselves and "Ham," the chimpanzee, who successfully transmitted signals from space (launched on this date in 1961) and your exploration of the moon.

31 OFFICIAL TIME BEGAN TO BE KEPT BY AN ATOMIC CLOCK
Celebrate by:
1. Find out about the first atomic clock, how accurate it is, and what purpose it serves.
2. Check the time of several watches to see how they vary.
3. Synchronize an electric digital clock and a wind-up clock at the beginning of the day. Have students predict which one will keep the more accurate time by the end of the school day. Assign a pair of students to check the correct time with the telephone company at the beginning and end of the school day. Check students' predictions.

January 1—NEW YEAR'S DAY
PAST AND FUTURE

Cut out the faces and fold on the dotted line.

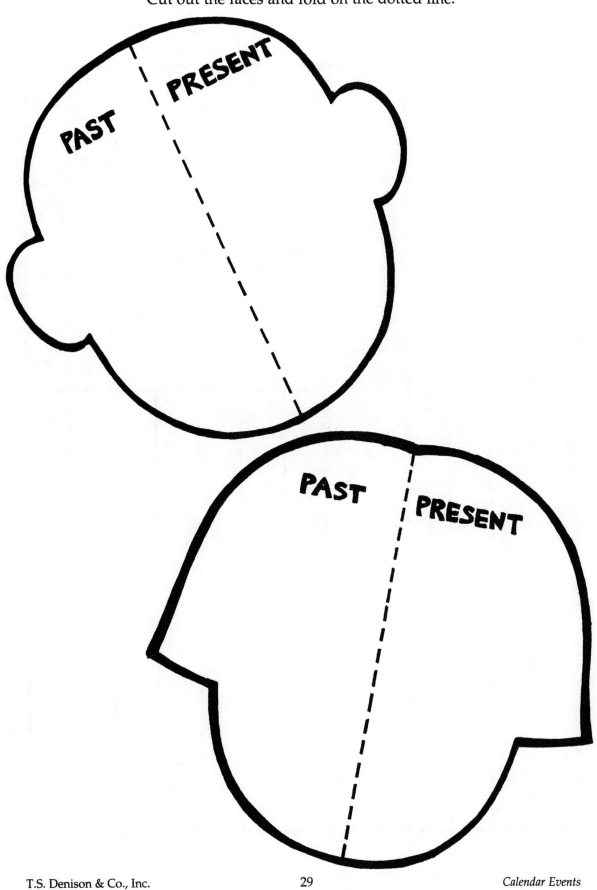

January 3—BETSY ROSS' BIRTHDAY
THE FIRST FLAG

Color the flag "r" for red, "b" for blue, and "w" for white.

January 18—SHARI LEWIS' BIRTHDAY
LAMBCHOP PUPPET

Color the puppet. Cut on the heavy lines. Make two.
Staple together around the edges, leaving the bottom open.

PAUL REVERE'S RIDE
Henry Wadsworth Longfellow

Listen my children, and you shall hear
Of the midnight ride of Paul Revere.
On the eighteenth of April, in seventy-five;
Hardly a man is now alive
Who remembers that famous day and year.
He said to his friend, "If the British march
By land or by sea from the town tonight,
Hang a lantern aloft in the belfry arch
Of the North Church tower as a signal light,
One, if by land, and two, if by sea:
And I on the opposite shore will be.
Ready to ride and spread the alarm
Through every Middlesex village and farm,
For the country folk to be up and to arm.

February

Flower – Primrose
Birthstone – Amethyst

February is the second month of the year. It has fewer days than any other month, even when it gets an extra day added to it in leap year. It is the only month whose length ever changes. February originally had thirty days until the time of Julius Caesar. February was not included in the first Roman calendar. When it was added it was the last month, but Caesar changed it to the second month.

MONTH

AMERICAN HEART MONTH
Celebrate by:
1. What is the shape, size and location of your heart? Where can we find the answers?
2. Locate a picture of the heart. Discuss the parts of the heart and ways to help insure a healthy heart.
3. Cut a heart from dark red construction paper. Cut a strip of red and blue paper, each 12 inches long. Accordion pleat both strips. Staple the strips to the heart to show the blue veins carrying blood to the heart and the red arteries carrying blood away from the heart.

BLACK HISTORY MONTH
Celebrate by:
1. Bring in pictures of famous African Americans. Identify the person and the reasons for which he or she is famous.
2. Design a poster which shows "justice for all people, regardless of race, creed or colors." (quote from Thurgood Marshall, first African American Supreme Court Justice)

HUMPBACK WHALE AWARENESS MONTH
Celebrate by:
1. Bring in pictures of different kinds of whales. Place the pictures on the bulletin board and write the appropriate name under each. Find out what they eat and where and when they migrate.
2. Compare whales to sharks.

CHILDREN'S DENTAL HEALTH MONTH
Celebrate by:
1. The slogan for Children's Dental Health Month is "Smile America." Can you come up with a better slogan?
2. Provide hand mirrors so students can "get to know their teeth." Have them count their teeth and find out the names of the teeth.
3. Ask a dentist to provide sample toothbrushes and visit the class demonstrating the correct way to brush the teeth. Your parent group may be willing to purchase toothbrushes and present a demonstration on caring for the teeth.

NATIONAL EMBROIDERY MONTH
Celebrate by:
1. Check with a parent or grandparent about visiting and sharing pieces of embroidery work. Ask him or her to give a demonstration.
2. Provide fabric, needles and embroidery thread for the class. Have the students draw or trace a simple design on a piece of fabric and then embroider it.

NATIONAL GRAPEFRUIT MONTH
Celebrate by:
1. Why are some grapefruits pink? In which states do grapefruit grow? Find out. Draw a picture tracing the grapefruit from seed to the table.
2. Cut a grapefruit, orange and lemon in half (all three are citrus fruits). Compare the inside and outside of the three.
3. Cut the fruit in small portions for a taste comparison test.

NATIONAL SNACK FOOD MONTH
Celebrate by:
1. Give students copies of "Snack Food 4 U" (page 41). After completing the page, discuss the choices. Decide on the five healthiest and the five unhealthiest foods from their lists.
2. Set out a variety of healthy snack foods. Place a card by each, listing a number such as 10 pretzel sticks, 5 almonds, 8 popcorn and 12 raisins. Give each student a small plastic bag and have them count the correct number of items and place in their bags. Have your snack under a tree or in a nearby park. Discuss taste and texture of the food items, how they grow and from what they are made.

NATIONAL PET OWNERS' MONTH
Celebrate by:
1. Ask how many students are pet owners. List the students' pets (or those of a neighbor or relative). Determine which is the most popular pet for the class.
2. Have each student decide which animal he or she thinks makes the best pet and write a paragraph telling why. Take turns reading about their choices.

WEEK

1st week NATIONAL NEW IDEA WEEK
Celebrate by:
1. Have each student make a headband and attach a cut-out light bulb (the symbol of an idea).
2. Have them wear the headbands as they "think" and then write down one idea for their school and one for their city. Include the purpose or benefit of the ideas. Read the ideas and decide if there are any practical and beneficial ones to implement. If so, send a copy to the principal and/or the mayor.

Week of 8th BOY SCOUTS OF AMERICA WEEK
Celebrate by:
1. If there are Boy Scouts (or Cub Scouts) in your class, ask them to wear their uniforms and share about the organization. Have them recite the Boy Scout Oath, explain their badges and how boys can join. A scout in an older class may be asked to do the above.
2. Make posters to promote Boy Scout Week and obtain permission to post them about the school.

2nd week NATIONAL KRAUT AND FRANKS WEEK
Celebrate by:
1. Write down what you think "kraut and franks" month means.
2. Serve kraut and franks (cut into small pieces). Heat in a microwave or electric skillet.

2nd week NEGRO HISTORY WEEK
Celebrate by:
1. Find out what country most of the "Negro" people came from to the United States. Locate the country on the map.
2. Check the library for history or biography books that deal with the early history of the "Negro" race.
3. How did the "Negro" people come to to the United States? Find out in which states they originally settled. Locate these states on a map.

3rd week NATIONAL BANANA WEEK
Celebrate by:
1. Draw a picture of bananas growing on a tree. Check a resource book to see if you drew the right kind of a tree and if your stalk of bananas is growing in the right direction!
2. Find out from which countries most of our bananas come—look for stickers on the bananas.
3. Bring in some green bananas. Watch how they turn yellow and ripen. Serve samples.
4. Bring in a few plantain (a type of banana), found in most food markets. Compare them to bananas. Peel, slice and fry them in an electric skillet with butter. Add brown sugar and cinnamon. Compare the taste with that of regular bananas.

3rd week NATIONAL DATE FESTIVAL WEEK
Celebrate by:
1. This festival is held annually in Indio, California. It is billed as "America's most unusual country fair." It features camel and ostrich races and an Arabian Nights Fantasy. Do you know of a country fair that is more unusual?
2. *Quiz:* Do dates grow on trees, bushes or small plants? How are dates harvested? How can we find out?
3. Dates are naturally sweet, no sweetener is added. Taste and compare samples of several different varieties.
4. Grow date seeds in paper cups filled with potting soil. Punch a drainage hole in the bottom of the cup. Place in a sunny spot. Do not overwater.

4th week NATIONAL PANCAKE WEEK

Celebrate by:

1. *See:* September 25, Pancake Day. Provide pancake mix, milk, butter and syrup. You will also need electric skillets or frying pans, spatulas, mixing bowls, measuring cups, paper plates, plastic knives and forks. Mix and measure as directed. Make square, round and triangular shaped pancakes.
2. Pour pancake mixture into squeeze bottles and let students make "their initials" pancakes.
3. Read the ingredients on the pancake mix box and discuss the contribution of each.
4. Read *The Pancake Man* by Eric Carle, and other books about pancakes.

DAY

1 NATIONAL FREEDOM DAY

Celebrate by:

1. *See:* 1st week of July, National Freedom Week. A Presidential Proclamation made on January 25, 1949 declared February 1 as National Freedom Day. How many years ago was the proclamation made? Who was the President at that time?
2. Have each student write an essay on what National Freedom Day means to him or her.

2 GROUNDHOG DAY

Celebrate by:

1. What is a groundhog? Are groundhogs real or imaginary? What is the old belief about the groundhog's shadow?
2. Bring in newspaper articles about groundhogs and Groundhog Day and share them with the class.
3. Make a puppet by first rolling a piece of tagboard into a cone. Tape the edges. Draw a groundhog on a piece of tagboard to a size that will fit into the cone. Tape the groundhog to one end of a pencil and push the other end through the hole in the bottom of the cone so it can be raised up and down.
4. Work in small groups to prepare a short skit to use with the puppet.

4 CHARLES LINDBERGH'S BIRTHDAY (1902–1974)

Celebrate by:

1. Charles Lindbergh was an American aviator who flew from New York, New York to Paris, France, nonstop, solo. Assign small groups one of the following questions to research. Have them write the questions and answers on 3" x 5" cards. How many miles did Lindbergh fly? What were the dates of the flight? How long did it take him? What was his nickname? How old was he when he made the flight? What was the name of his plane? What was the amount of the prize money he won?
2. Find or copy pictures of Lindbergh and his plane. Place them on the bulletin board. Add the 3" x 5" cards to the bulletin board.

5 WEATHERMAN'S DAY

Celebrate by:

1. This date commemorates the birth of one of America's first weathermen, John Jeffries. Watch or tape a TV weather report to show to the class. Discuss the report.
2. Give each student a copy of the "Weather Prediction Chart" (page 42). Have them predict the weather for the next three days. At the end of each day, check the predictions against the actual weather.
3. Older children can add daily high and low temperature predictions to their charts and then check the temperature at the beginning and end of each school day.

6 CHINA: LANTERN DAY

Celebrate by:

1. A lantern procession marks the end of the Chinese lunar calendar year. Invite a parent, neighbor or friend, who can explain the Chinese New Year, to visit your class.
2. Copy the "Chinese Lantern" pattern (page 43) onto different colored construction paper. Have students each make a lantern. Younger students will enjoy a parade around the classroom or playground carrying their lanterns.

6 BABE RUTH'S BIRTHDAY (1895–1948)

Celebrate by:

1. Babe Ruth was a left-handed pitcher who hit 714 home runs. He played in ten World Series games. What was his real name? Invite students to bring in baseball cards featuring pitchers.
2. Check the cards to see how many of the pitchers are left-handed. Older students can compare pitching statistics.
3. Play a game of baseball at recess or Physical Education period.

MASSACHUSETTS ADMISSION DAY

Celebrate by:

1. Massachusetts became the 6th state in 1788. Add this information to your United States map (page 13). Color the state lightly with colored pencil or crayon.
2. Write this state opposite its number on the Admission Page (page 15).

7 CHARLES DICKENS' BIRTHDAY (1812–1870)

Celebrate by:

1. *See:* December 25, Christmas Day. Find out about this man—who was he? For what is he best known? Where did he live?
2. Have students locate some of his other books, read them and give an overview.

11 THOMAS ALVA EDISON'S BIRTHDAY (1847–1931)

Celebrate by:

1. Thomas Edison invented the light bulb. What would it be like today if the electric light bulb had not been invented?
2. Have each student draw a floor plan of his or her house. Count the number of electric light bulbs in each room. Mark the location of each light bulb and write the number in each room beside that room. Total the numbers.

12 ABRAHAM LINCOLN'S BIRTHDAY (1809–1865)

Celebrate by:

1. Lincoln's son, Tad, kept his cat, Tabby, at the White House. See how many cats and dogs (and their names), that were members of White House families, your students can discover. List them on a classroom chart.
2. Acquire as many sets of Lincoln Logs as possible. Have small groups construct log cabins.
3. Locate a copy of the Gettysburg Address (in encyclopedia or history book). Make copies and have students each take turns reading a line or two.

13 FIRST MAGAZINE PUBLISHED IN AMERICA (1741)

Celebrate by:

1. The first magazine published in America was "The American Magazine," published by Andrew Bradford. It was published three days before Benjamin Franklin's "General Magazine." Check out a selection of children's magazines from the school or public library. Allow time for students to read.
2. Discuss the different types—science, history, astronomy—and what kind of materials can be found in magazines—fiction, nonfiction, poems, puzzles.
3. Make a copy of "Inside Magazines" (page 44) for each student.

14 ARIZONA ADMISSION DAY

Celebrate by:

1. Arizona became the 48th state in 1912. Add this information to your United States map (page 13). Color the state lightly with colored pencil or crayon.
2. Write this state opposite its number on the State Admission Order page (page 15).

14 GEORGE WASHINGTON GALE FERRIS' BIRTHDAY (1859–1896)

Celebrate by:

1. Write the man's name on the chalkboard. Instruct students to look carefully at the name. After about twenty seconds, ask why they think this might be a day to celebrate (he invented the Ferris Wheel in 1893).
2. Have students share experiences of Ferris Wheels.
3. Provide construction materials such as Tinker Toys and Erector Sets and have small groups work to construct a Ferris Wheel.

14 OREGON ADMISSION DAY

Celebrate by:

1. Oregon became the 33rd state in 1859. Add this information to your United States map (page 13). Color the state lightly with colored pencil or crayon.
2. Write this state opposite its number on the State Admission Order page (page 15).

14 VALENTINE'S DAY

Celebrate by:

1. Have students decorate valentine cookies. Wrap each cookie in colored plastic wrap. Make envelopes from red paper. Have students place the cookies inside the envelopes along with a note telling a little about themselves. Send or deliver the valentines to the children's ward of a local hospital (or a facility for children who live away from home).
2. Arrange with a facility for older people for a list of names of the residents. Give each student a name and have them make a valentine for that person. As a class project, decorate a valentine box. Place the valentines inside the box, visit the facility, and have students take turns drawing a name from the box and calling out the name. Have each student introduce themselves to the recipient of the valentine.
3. To make a valentine mouse, make copies of "Valentine Mouse"(page 45) on red construction paper for the students. Instruct each student to keep the paper folded and cut and glue a heart-shaped eye and ear in place. Staple a piece of yarn to the mouse for a tail. If desired, a message can be written inside the mouse.

15 SUSAN B. (BROWNELL) ANTHONY DAY (1820–1906)

Celebrate by:

1. Susan B. Anthony helped women get the vote. She was arrested and fined for voting in 1872. What would it be like today if women could not vote? Assign small groups to discuss this question and then present their views to the class.
2. Give each student a copy of "The Short Life of a Coin" (page 46). After completing the work sheet, show a Susan B. Anthony coin and another silver dollar. Compare the two.
    Answers: 1. dollar 2. 1979 3. 86 4. no

17 NATIONAL P.T.A. FOUNDER'S DAY (1897)

Celebrate by:

1. Find out the name of your P.T.A. president and other board members. Discuss what this organization has done for your school and class this school year.
2. Invite a board member to speak to your class about the work of the organization.
3. Write thank-you notes, draw thank-you pictures or make a long classroom letter, with each student adding a note, and send it to your P.T.A.

18 PLANET PLUTO DISCOVERED (1930)

Celebrate by:

1. Pluto is the most recently discovered planet. Find the names of the other planets.
2. Cut paper circles in sizes that correspond to the size of each planet. Paste them to a piece of paper—smallest to largest. Write the planet's correct name on each circle.

20 FIRST AMERICAN TO ORBIT THE EARTH

Celebrate by:

1. John Glenn, Jr., was the first American and the third man to orbit the earth. What was the date? (1962) What was the name of the capsule? (Friendship–7) How many orbits did he complete? (3) What was the name of the spacecraft? (Mercury–Atlas 6)
2. Find out the name of the first man to orbit the earth and the date this took place. From what country did the man come? Find that country on a map.

22 LORD BADEN POWELL'S BIRTHDAY (1857–1941)
Celebrate by:
1. *See:* Week of February 8th, Boy Scouts of America Week. Lord Baden Powell, founder of the Boy Scouts and the Girl Guides, was born in London, England. Find his birthplace on a map.
2. Find out how old he was when he founded the Boy Scouts, and how old he was when he died. How many years after founding the Boy Scouts did he die?

22 GEORGE WASHINGTON'S BIRTHDAY (1732–1799)
Celebrate by:
1. Have students work in small groups and plan a skit on one incident in George Washington's life. Present the skit to the class.
2. Provide baked tart shells (or ask a parent to bake them) and cherry pie filling. Have students "make" their own "George Washington" cherry pie tart.

24 WILHELM GRIMM'S BIRTHDAY (1786–1859)
Celebrate by:
1. Wilhelm and his brother, Jacob (*see:* January 4), collected fairy tales. The were born in Hanau, Germany (near Frankfurt) and died in Berlin, Germany. Find Germany on the map and then locate the two cities.
2. How many years did each brother live? Who was the oldest? Who lived the longest?
3. Read a fairy tale from one in the Grimm Brothers' collection, then read a modern version of the same story and compare the two.

26 GRAND CANYON NATIONAL PARK
Celebrate by:
1. Grand Canyon National Park was established in 1919 by an act of Congress. It is mainly in the state of Arizona. Locate the park on a map. Which states border Arizona? What is the name of the river that runs through the Grand Canyon?
2. Locate a picture or two of the Grand Canyon. Read about it and discuss its formation. Provide colored chalk or finger paint for students to create their own visual concept of the Grand Canyon.

29 LEAP YEAR
Celebrate by:
1. Leap year occurs in every year which can be divided equally by four (except the years that mark the even hundred). The only century leap years are those that can be divided evenly by 400. How many days does February usually have? How many days does February have in a leap year?
2. Challenge students to find out why leap year was added to the calendar.
3. State the following: If you were born ten years ago on February 29, how many birthdays would you have had?
4. Have students write down the following dates: 1992, 1996, 1999. Have them figure out which years are leap years.
5. Have students write down the following dates: 1200, 1600, 1900, 2000. Which of these century years are leap years?

Name _____

February, Month—NATIONAL SNACK FOOD MONTH
SNACK FOOD 4 U

List five healthy snack foods.

1. _____
2. _____
3. _____
4. _____
5. _____

List five unhealthy snack foods.

1. _____
2. _____
3. _____
4. _____
5. _____

Draw a picture of your favorite snack food.

My favorite snack food is _____.

Name _____

February 5 – WEATHERMAN'S DAY
WEATHER PREDICTION CHART

Predict the weather for the next three days. Use a blue crayon to circle your predictions. At the end of the day, circle the actual weather with a red crayon.

1. Date: _____

Cloud cover:	none	little	cloudy	very cloudy
Temperature:	hot	warm	cold	very cold
Conditions:	rain	snow	wind	other _____

2. Date: _____

Cloud cover:	none	little	cloudy	very cloudy
Temperature:	hot	warm	cold	very cold
Conditions:	rain	snow	wind	other _____

3. Date: _____

Cloud cover:	none	little	cloudy	very cloudy
Temperature:	hot	warm	cold	very cold
Conditions:	rain	snow	wind	other _____

Fold on the dotted line. Cut on the solid lines. Overlap the edges of the paper and tape in place. Cut a 12-inch strip of paper and staple the ends to opposite sides of the lantern for a handle.

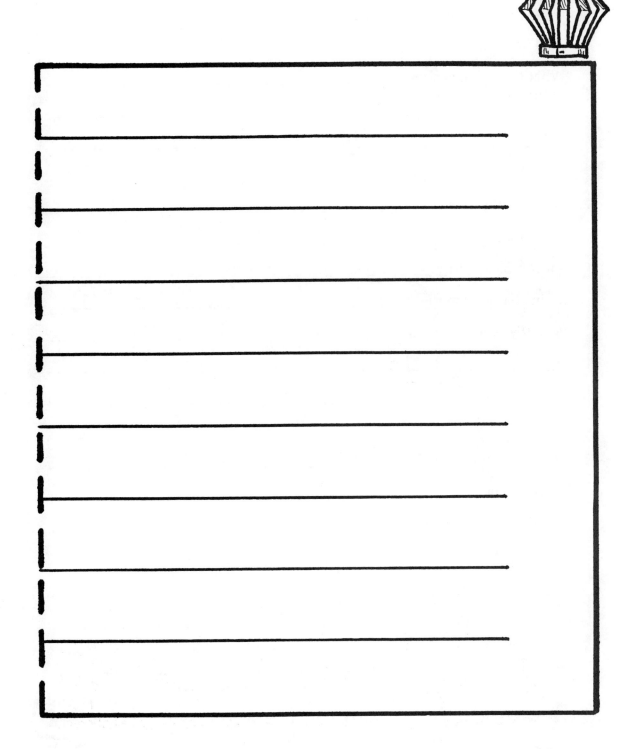

February 13 – FIRST MAGAZINE PUBLISHED IN AMERICA
INSIDE MAGAZINES

Look through magazines and find an example of each item listed. Read the item and answer the questions.

1. Name of the magazine:_____

   Title of a poem: _____

   What the poem is about: _____

   _____

   _____

2. Name of the magazine:_____

   Title of a story: _____

   Author of the story:_____

   Main character in the story:_____

   What the story is about: _____

   _____

   _____

3. Title of a nonfiction article: _____

   Name of the author: _____

   Name of the magazine:_____

   What the article is about: _____

   _____

   _____

February 14 – VALENTINE'S DAY
VALENTINE MOUSE

Fold the paper on the dotted line and cut the valentine. Cut two valentine ears and glue to each side of the open side of the large end of the valentine. Draw a nose and eyes. Staple a yarn tail to the pointed end.

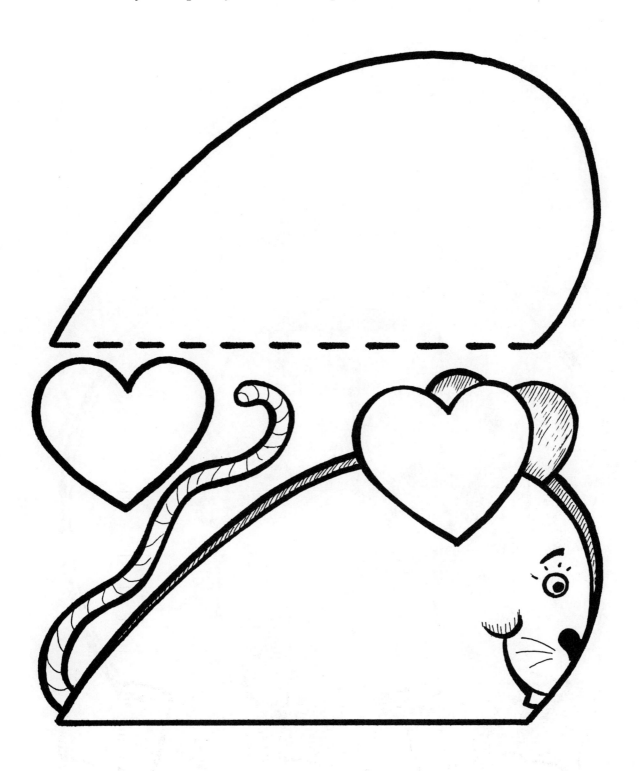

Name _____

February 15 – SUSAN B. ANTHONY DAY
THE SHORT LIFE OF A COIN

The first woman to have her likeness on an American coin was Susan B. Anthony. She was born in 1820 and died in 1906.

Circle the correct answers.

1. What coin was it?   quarter   half-dollar   dollar

2. When was the coin first issued?   1901   1950   1979

3. How old was she when she died?   68   86   90

4. Did she live to see the coin?   yes   no

March

Flower – Violet
Birthstone – Aquamarine

March is the third month of the year, however, it was the first month of the ancient Roman calendar. March has thirty-one days. March brings us spring. This month has no national holidays.

MONTH

Regarding March, you often hear, "in like a lion and out like a lamb." Ask the students for their interpretation of the saying.

NATIONAL BABY MONTH
Celebrate by:
1. Find out how many students have a baby in their family. Tally the boy and girl babies and make a picture graph. Have students draw heads of babies to represent each one.
2. Invite students to each bring in their baby pictures. Tape the photographs to the bulletin board and assign a number to each. Have students identify class members from the photographs by writing the person's name opposite the number on the sheet of paper.
3. Have each student find out his or her birth weight and length. Measure and weigh each student. Have each determine the difference between the birth weight and length and today's weight and height.

NATIONAL FOOT HEALTH MONTH
Celebrate by:
1. Have students trace around their shoes on pieces of paper, then remove their shoes and trace around their feet on other pieces of paper. Next, have them cut out the feet tracings and place inside the drawings of their shoes. Ask if they feel they are wearing the right size shoes and why they think so.
2. Estimate the number of bones in each foot and in each hand. Provide a skeletal picture of a hand and foot or obtain an X-ray from a podiatrist or other source. Check the correct number against estimates. Discuss the similarities and differences between the two skeletal structures—hand and foot.
3. Provide pans of finger paint and water and a large sheet of butcher paper and paper towels. Have students make their "paint footprints" close together on the paper to form a footprint collage.

NATIONAL FROZEN FOOD MONTH
Celebrate by:
1. Provide either a fruit or vegetable in the following states—fresh, canned and frozen. Compare the similarities and differences.
2. Add one half cup of water to each of three paper cups. Add two tablespoons of sugar to one cup and two tablespoons of salt to another cup. Stir until dissolved. Add an equal amount of fruit to each container. Place the cups in the freezer for a few hours. Predict what will happen to each cup of fruit. When frozen, remove the three cups from the freezer and discuss the experiment.

NATIONAL MUSIC IN OUR SCHOOLS' MONTH

Celebrate by:

1. Introduce chants and ballads to the class. Assign small groups to each create a chant or ballad.
2. Years ago, minstrels and troubadours traveled and entertained. Have the groups practice their ballads while walking.
3. Arrange to have the class present their original ballads to another class, on the playground or during lunch.

NATIONAL NOODLE MONTH

Celebrate by:

1. Ask for a definition of pasta and how many different kinds students think there are. Have students bring in a piece of pasta in any form. Glue each piece to a 3" x 5" card and write the name of it on the card. Add to the collection as students make new discoveries.
2. Make egg noodles. Work in small groups. Beat an egg (one egg for every five students) until foamy. Gradually add flour until the mixture is very stiff. Roll into a ball, and then roll out on a floured board. Roll as thin as possible. Cut into thin strips. Allow to dry for about an hour. Carefully drop the noodles into boiling water and cook about fifteen minutes. Drain and serve with salt, pepper, butter, and grated cheese.

    Invite parents to help with the "noodle making" and to provide ingredients, rolling pins, wax paper, electric frying pans, plates, and forks.

NATIONAL NUTRITION MONTH

Celebrate by:

1. Make a giant-size food pyramid using different colors of butcher paper for each section. Have students bring in pictures of food from newspaper or magazine ads (or paint them) and paste the food in the proper section.
2. Arrange to place the food pyramid in the cafeteria.
3. Have students bring in a collection of empty, clean food containers. Check the containers for nutritional content. Sort the containers into three groups—those with high, medium, and low nutritional value.

NATIONAL PEANUT MONTH

Celebrate by:

1. *See:* November 12, Peanut Butter Invented and January 5, George Washington Carver's Death Anniversary.

    Hide peanuts around the room before the students arrive. As each student finds a peanut (they can only find one), have the student write his or her name on the chalkboard. After all the peanuts are found, have students carefully break the largest end from their peanuts. Remove and eat the peanuts. Save the shells.
2. To make a peanut into a finger puppet, decorate a peanut shell with bits of felt, paper, lace or other items from the art box. Add facial features and place it on the end of a finger.
3. Divide into small groups and create a poem, skit or song to be used with the puppets. Present to the class.
4. Bring in a favorite peanut butter recipe. Tape the recipes around the room so those who wish may copy them.

5. Have each student cut a large peanut shape from tan paper and on the peanut write an interesting fact, riddle or poem about peanuts. Post the "peanuts" on the bulletin board.
6. Set out a jar of peanuts in the shell. Tape the lid securely. Have students estimate the number of peanuts in the jar and then write their names with their estimates on a chart. Assign a small group to open the jar and count the peanuts. Have another group divide the peanuts equally among the class members.

NATIONAL POETRY MONTH
Celebrate by:
1. Have students bring in and read their favorite poems.
2. Have students each bring in a story book written in rhyme. Compare the books.
3. Assign, or let each student choose, a poem of eight lines or more to memorize. Recite a few each day.

NATIONAL RED CROSS MONTH
Celebrate by:
1. *See:* May 8, World Red Cross Day; May 21, Red Cross Founding Anniversary; December 25, Clara Barton.
2. Find out why the red cross is the symbol of this organization. Ask if anyone has or knows someone who has been assisted by the Red Cross, or someone who works for the Red Cross.
3. Invite a Red Cross worker to speak to your class.

NATIONAL WOMEN'S HISTORY MONTH
Celebrate by:
1. Brainstorm names of women in history, past and present. List the names on a chart.
2. Divide the class into groups. Have each group decide on one of the women to research and report on her contributions.
3. Consider women in your community who have made a significant contribution to your community. Have each student write a letter of appreciation to one of these women.

NATIONAL YOUTH ART MONTH
Celebrate by:
1. Make a painting using any medium or technique. Make a frame for the painting (from a cardboard box, drinking straws, yarn) and sign the painting.
2. Take turns displaying the painting on an easel for an hour. Have the artist explain the medium and technique used.
3. After the classroom show, make arrangements to display the students' art in a local bank, library or mall.

1st week IRISH HERITAGE WEEK

Celebrate by:

1. Find Ireland on the world map. Locate the capital.
2. Find out if any students are of Irish descent. Invite a member from the student's family to visit class and share photographs, art work, handicrafts, or food dishes with the class.
3. Teach students an Irish dance.

1st week NEWSPAPER EDUCATION WEEK

Celebrate by:

1. Ask your newspaper office for enough day-old copies of the newspaper for your class. Allow time for students to browse through the newspaper. Locate the headlines, editorials, names of the publisher and other staff people, by-lined articles, weather reports and letters to the editor.
2. Assign students to write a practice letter to the editor about an important concern.
3. Study the classified section and then have students write an ad for something they would like to sell.

1st week PHYSICAL EDUCATION AND SPORTS' WEEK

Celebrate by:

1. Introduce and practice a new motor skill each day of the week such as hop, jump, skip, gallop, and leap.
2. Have small groups work on skills or endurance goals that they feel would be a realistic accomplishment for their age. Decide which of the goals would aid in physical development and implement them.
3. With input from the students, decide on three games or activities to play during recess. Set up three groups and each day have students rotate among the activities.

1st week SCHOOL BREAKFAST WEEK

Celebrate by:

1. Work in small groups to plan an attractive, healthy breakfast. Vote on the "best" breakfast menu. Ask your cafeteria manager to cast his or her vote.
2. Plan the food needed, purchase the food and prepare the breakfast in the classroom.

2nd week GIRL SCOUT WEEK (1912)

Celebrate by:

1. *See:* October 31, Juliette Low's Birthday. If there are Girl Scouts or Brownies in the class, have them share their uniforms, tell how they earn badges, and recite the Girl Scout oath.
2. Have the Scouts share the community projects in which they are involved and discuss camps they have attended.

3rd week AMERICAN CHOCOLATE WEEK

Celebrate by:

1. *Quiz:* Does chocolate come from the leaves, seeds, or stem of a plant? Is the plant a tree, vine, bush, or root? (Cocoa is a powder made by grinding the seeds of the cacao tree.)
2. Make hot chocolate using cocoa, sugar and milk. Make chocolate chip cookies.

3rd week NATIONAL POISON PREVENTION WEEK
Celebrate by:
1. About 2 million people suffer from poisoning each year; of these, 10,000 result in deaths.
2. Draw a picture of the symbol we see on containers that tell us the contents are poisonous.
3. Discuss what to do to prevent poisoning—people, pets and the environment.
4. Discuss how to treat a person who has been poisoned by swallowing, inhaling or spilling a poisonous substance on their hands.
5. Many plants are poisonous to small children, pets and adults. On a classroom chart, list as many of these plants as students can discover.

4th week NATIONAL ART WEEK
Celebrate by:
1. Have students illustrate a book jacket for a favorite book.
2. Make plans to visit an art gallery, an art show or to visit an artist in his or her studio.

3rd week NATIONAL WILDLIFE WEEK
Celebrate by:
1. Decorate bulletin boards to represent a jungle, ocean, forest and prairie. Have students bring in pictures of their favorite wildlife animals and add to the appropriate habitat.
2. Keep a log recording all the wildlife seen in one day or in one week.
3. Write a short story about a wild animal the student has never seen but would like to see.

4th week SCHOOL LIBRARY MEDIA CENTER WEEK
Celebrate by:
1. Ask if students know what a Library Media Center is. Arrange to visit your school media center. Ask the media specialist to explain his or her position and tell about the job as a career potential.
2. Write a letter to the media specialist telling what was learned during the visit to the media center.

DAY

1 NATIONAL PIG DAY
Celebrate by:
1. Although pigs are kept by some people as pets, pigs provide a variety of sources for meat. Make a list of meats (pork) that come from pigs.
2. Write a paragraph about what it would be like to have a pig as a house pet.
3. Pigs have played important roles in literature. Can you think of some pigs who were important characters in stories, poems and nursery rhymes?

1 NEBRASKA ADMISSION DAY
Celebrate by:
1. Nebraska became the 37th state in 1867. Add this information to your United States map (page 13). Color the state lightly with a colored pencil or crayon.
2. Write this state opposite its number on the State Admission Order page (page 15).

1 OHIO ADMISSION DAY

Celebrate by:

1. Ohio became the 17th state in 1803. Add this information to your United States map (page 13). Color the state lightly with a colored pencil or crayon.
2. Write this state opposite its number on the State Admission Order page (page 15).

2 DR. SEUSS' BIRTHDAY (1904–1991)

Celebrate by:

1. Bring in a selection of Dr. Seuss books. Allow time for silent reading.
2. Ask students to share their favorite Dr. Seuss book and why they prefer it.
3. Take a vote to find the majority's choice.
4. Give each student a copy of "Do You Know Dr. Seuss? (page 57) to complete.

3 ALEXANDER GRAHAM BELL'S BIRTHDAY

Celebrate by:

1. Mr. Bell invented the telephone. Discuss how people communicated before his invention.
2. What would it be like today if we did not have a telephone system? Make a list of other ways we could send a message if we did not have telephones.
3. Have students work in pairs to make a tin can telephone. Have each pair bring in two cans the same size, with lids safely removed, and a small hole punched in the bottom of each can. Provide long lengths of string. Instruct students how to thread the ends of the strings between the two cans and through the holes in the cans. Tie a knot in the end of each string inside the cans. Separate from partners so the strings are stretched tight. Have students turn their backs to each other and talk through their tin can phones.

3 FLORIDA ADMISSION DAY

Celebrate by:

1. Florida became the 27th state in 1845. Add this information to your United States map (page 13). Color the state lightly with a colored pencil or crayon.
2. Write this state opposite its number on the State Admission Order page (page 15).

3 NATIONAL ANTHEM DAY (1931)

Celebrate by:

1. A national anthem is the official song of a country. Congress did not adopt our national anthem until 1931. However, it was recognized as our national anthem many years before by both the army and the navy. What is the name of our national anthem?
2. Find out when and where it was written, who wrote the words, and who wrote the music.
3. Read all the verses to the class and then sing, as a group, the first verse.
4. Students who were born or lived in another country may know that country's national anthem. Ask them to either sing it or recite the words.

4 VERMONT ADMISSION DAY

Celebrate by:

1. Vermont became the 14th state in 1791. Add this information to your United States map (page 13). Color the state lightly with a colored pencil or crayon.
2. Write this state opposite its number on the State Admission Order page (page 15).

1st Friday WORLD DAY OF PRAYER

Celebrate by:

1. People all over the world pause and pray annually on the first Friday of March. Ask students to think about the needs of our world, our country or someone they know. Take time for silent prayer.
2. Find out how the churches in your community are celebrating this day.

10 AMERIGO VESPUCCI'S BIRTHDAY (1454–1512)

Celebrate by:

1. Some people believe that this man was the first to reach the "New World." Divide the class into two groups—those who agree and those who disagree. Have them do research on Amerigo Vespucci and then have a debate.
2. Pin a world map to the bulletin board. Use blue yarn to outline Vespucci's voyage, and red yarn to show the voyage of Columbus. Pin the yarn to the board.

10 SALVATION ARMY FOUNDED IN THE UNITED STATES (1880)

Celebrate by:

1. What comes to mind when you hear "The Salvation Army"?
2. Most students are familiar with the Salvation Army through the people who ring bells at Christmas time, and are unaware of all the work they do. Check the Yellow Pages of the telephone directory for the nearest Salvation Army office and ask about having a representative come to class and share about their organization.

10 PAPER MONEY ISSUED

Celebrate by:

1. The first paper money in the United States, consisting of five, ten and twenty dollar bills, was issued on this date in 1886. Have each student write down all the denominations printed today.
2. Challenge older students to name the person whose picture appears on each bill.
3. Research the changes that have taken place in paper money since it was first issued.
4. Check with a parent or friend who may be able to share money from another country. Compare the size, color and value with our paper money.
5. Give small groups a fairly new one dollar bill and a magnifying glass. Have students locate the serial number, treasury seal, date printed, Great Seal of the United States, and a signature.

12 GIRL SCOUT FOUNDING ANNIVERSARY
See: October 31, Juliette Low's Birthday.

13 PLANET URANUS DISCOVERED
Celebrate by:
1. Have students find out when Uranus was discovered (1781) and who the astronomer was who discovered it (Sir William Hershel).
2. Locate pictures of the planets. List the planets in order to show their distance from the sun—nearest to farthest.

13 UNCLE SAM'S BIRTHDAY (1830)
Celebrate by:
1. Uncle Sam is a figure that symbolizes the United States. Have students find out when and where the symbol originated, and locate pictures of how the symbol has changed throughout the years.
2. Uncle Sam first appeared as a cartoon figure in the 1830s. Have students draw a cartoon to illustrate a modern-day Uncle Sam.

14 INTERNATIONAL DAY OF THE SEAL
Celebrate by:
1. Ask students for attributes in identifying a seal. Assign small groups to research one of the following: seal, sea lion, walrus, porpoise, and then use the information to compare the animals.
2. Make a "Save the Seals" poster.

2nd Sunday PLANT A FLOWER DAY
Celebrate by:
1. Discuss ways flowers are propagated such as seeds, cuttings, tubers, and bulbs.
2. Have students each bring in a flower seed (and if possible a matching flower or flower picture). Place the seeds in the bottom section of egg cartons. Use toothpick banners to identify each seed. Push the toothpicks into the edges of the egg cups.
3. Discuss and examine the parts of a flower. Give each student a copy of "Where Is It?" (page 58), magnifying glasses and a flower to examine. Ask parents to provide flowers or check with a flower stand for their day-old flowers.
4. Plant the flower seeds the students brought to class.

15 MAINE ADMISSION DAY
Celebrate by:
1. Maine became the 23rd state in 1820. Add this information to your United States map (page 13). Color the state lightly with a colored pencil or crayon.
2. Write this state opposite its number on the State Admission Order page (page 15).

17 BOYS AND GIRLS CAMP FIRE FOUNDING DAY (1910)

Celebrate by:

1. First called Camp Fire Girls. If there are any members in the class, ask them to share about the organization. If not, find out about this group.
2. Compare Camp Fire Boys and Girls to Boy and Girl Scouts. Note the similarities and differences.

17 ST. PATRICK'S DAY

Celebrate by:

1. Discuss the different colors of potatoes and of snakes. Use colored playdough to make a potato and a snake.
2. Find out why these two symbols, as well as the shamrock and the color green, are associated with St. Patrick's Day.
3. Have each student bring in one green fruit or one green vegetable—apples, celery, cabbage, bell peppers. Provide napkins and plastic picnic knives. Cut the food items into sample pieces for a taste comparison.
4. Give each student a copy of "Wee Bit of Ireland" (page 59) to complete.
   Answers: 1. potato; 2. Dublin; 3. Patrick; 4. shamrock; 5. green; 6. leprechaun; 7. jig; 8. stew

19 U.S. STANDARD TIME ACT (1918)

Celebrate by:

1. On this date, Congress passed the standard time act which established standard time zones for the United States. In which time zone do you live? See if students can name the other time zones.
2. Provide copies of "Standard Time Zone Map" (page 60) for each student. Locate and discuss the time zones. Have students complete the activity page.

20 or 21 SPRING BEGINS

Celebrate by:

1. The day for the beginning of spring is marked by the vernal equinox. Find out what this means.
2. Have the students write a poem about spring.
3. Have the students write a paragraph about their favorite season.

22 MARCEL MARCEAU'S BIRTHDAY (1923 –)

Celebrate by:

1. Ask if anyone knows why we would celebrate this man's birthday. This actor/pantomimist, known for his mime acts, was born in France. Discuss the art of mime.
2. Have students make white paper plate mime faces. Staple the plates to the tops of heavy cardboard strip handles to make stick puppet faces.
3. Work in small groups to make mime presentations.

25 GERTZON BORGLUM'S BIRTHDAY (1867–1941)

Celebrate by:

1. See if anyone knows who this man was and why we would celebrate his birthday. (He was the sculptor for Mount Rushmore.)
2. Mount Rushmore is located in the Black Hills of South Dakota. Locate the spot on a map.
3. The faces of four American presidents are carved on Mount Rushmore. Find out the names of those presidents. Discuss why these four may have been chosen.
4. Provide clay or playdough for students to sculpt "a face on a mountain."

30 DOCTOR'S DAY

Celebrate by:

1. Have students write down as many different kinds of doctors as they can think of and then write them on a classroom chart.
2. Assign small groups to each interview a different doctor who is a specialist in a particular field. Make a report to the class.
3. Invite a doctor to speak to the class about the educational requirements in becoming a doctor.

31 EIFFEL TOWER ANNIVERSARY (1889)

Celebrate by:

1. The Eiffel Tower was completed on this date in 1889. It was designed by Gustave Eiffel and stands 1,000 feet high. At the time it was built, it was the tallest structure in the world. Where is the Eiffel Tower located? Why was it built? For what is it used today?
2. Ask if anyone has visited the sight or knows someone who has that may have photographs, posters or souvenirs to share.
3. Research the height and date of completion for the Empire State Building, World Trade Center, Sears Tower, and any high rise building in your city or state.
4. Have students draw pictures of themselves standing beside the Eiffel Tower.
5. Display a picture of the Eiffel Tower. Use unit blocks to construct an Eiffel Tower. Older students can use a scale of one block being equal to 50 or 100 feet (height).
6. Make a time line to show both the height and the date construction was completed for the Eiffel Tower and the buildings in #3 above.

March 2 – DR. SEUSS' BIRTHDAY
DO YOU KNOW DR. SEUSS?

1. Dr. Seuss was a pseudonym, or a name used specifically for his children's books. What was this author's real name? _____

2. Look in the thesaurus and dictionary to see how many words you can find that mean the same as a pseudonym. _____
_____
_____

3. When was Dr. Seuss born? _____

4. When did he die? _____

5. In what state had he been living when he died? _____

6. What was the title of the author's first book for children? _____
_____

7. What was the copyright date of his first book? _____

8. List three unusual things about Dr. Seuss' books.
   a) _____
   _____
   _____

   b) _____
   _____
   _____

   c) _____
   _____
   _____

2nd Sunday in March —PLANT A FLOWER DAY
WHERE IS IT?

Draw a line from the word to the matching part of the flower.

corolla (petals)

anther

sepals

stigma

ovary

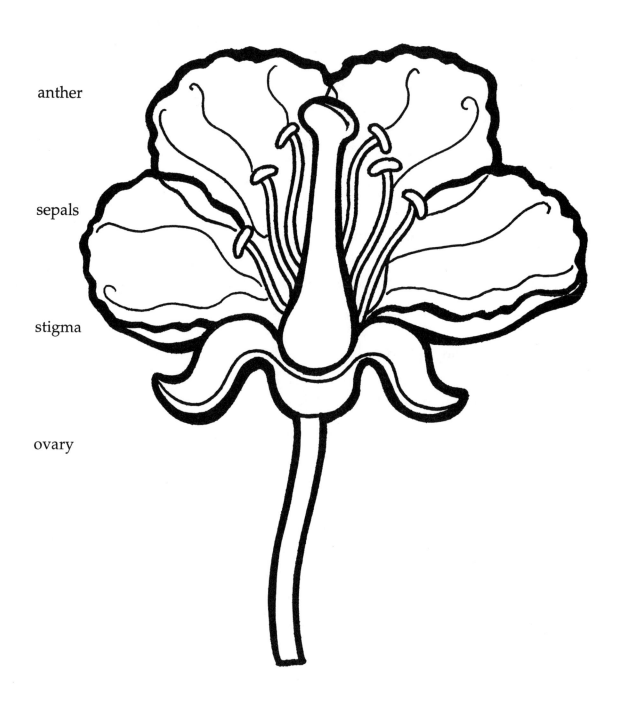

March 17 – ST. PATRICK'S DAY
WEE BIT OF IRELAND

Many people living in America came from Ireland. Others can trace their roots back to the Emerald Isle. Write the correct Irish answer in the space.

Name _____

March 19 – U.S. STANDARD TIME ACT
STANDARD TIME ZONE MAP

Lightly color each time zone a different color.

1. In which time zone do you live?_____

2. In which time zone is the state east (or west) of you? _____

3. In which time zone is the west coast? _____

4. In which time zone is Florida? _____

5. Find and list the name of a state that is in two different time zones. In which time zones is it? _____

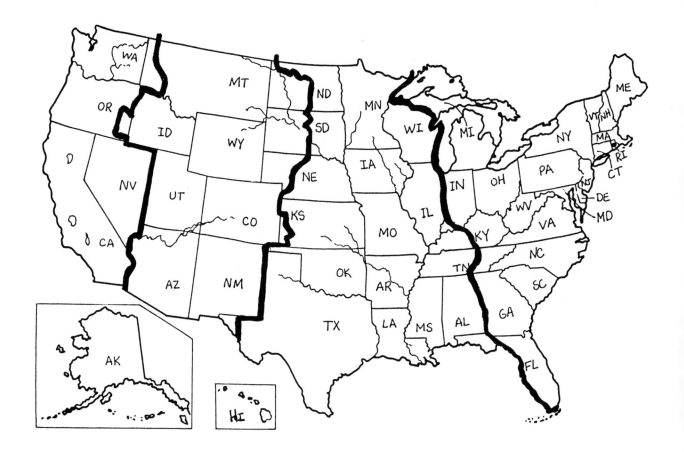

April

Flower – Sweet pea and daisy
Birthstone – Diamond

April is the fourth month of the year. In an early Roman calendar, it was the second month. April became the 4th month when Caesar established the Julian calendar in 46 B.C. Easter usually comes in April. April also brings spring with new plant and animal life.

MONTH

CANCER CONTROL MONTH
Celebrate by:
1. Divide the class into three groups. Assign groups to interview a dermatologist, a nutritionist and a pediatrician about ways to help prevent cancer.
2. From the interviews, compile a class chart to show what students can do to lower their risk of cancer.

KEEP AMERICA BEAUTIFUL MONTH
Celebrate by:
1. Make a poster for Keep America Beautiful Month. Take the posters on a visit to other classrooms and enlist their help in keeping your school and yard beautiful.
2. Take on a project such as keeping a part of the school yard free of litter, planting flowers or sweeping walks.
3. Check with your city to see if there is a project your entire school could undertake such as cleaning litter from a park, walking trail or beach area. Invite the principal to class to discuss the project and how you plan to implement it. Present the final plans to the school and enlist the help of students and staff.

MATHEMATICS EDUCATION MONTH
Celebrate by:
1. On a chart, list other names for mathematics—math, numbers, arithmetic.
2. Using manipulatives, introduce easy examples of addition, subtraction, multiplication, division, and fractions.
3. Explain algebra and geometry in simple terms.
4. Challenge students to each improve their math scores during this month.

NATIONAL GARDEN MONTH
Celebrate by:
1. Start a garden in the classroom such as pot, window box, or cup gardens.
2. Purchase climbing vegetable seeds and start them in large pots. Have students use their ideas to create structures for the plants to climb.
3. Select a plot of ground next to your classroom. Have students work together to plan, prepare, plant, and care for a small outdoor garden.
4. Have each student keep a daily log of the gardening activities in which he or she is involved.

PREVENTION OF ANIMAL CRUELTY MONTH
Celebrate by:
1. Discuss what students could do if they see anyone being unkind to animals.
2. Discuss ways to treat animals kindly.
3. Visit the local animal shelter, Humane Society or a veterinarian's office.

WEEK

1st week NATIONAL DANCE WEEK
Celebrate by:
1. Introduce a simple dance such as forming a circle, clapping hands, and then taking turns (or with a partner) free dancing inside the circle.
2. Invite a parent to teach a folk dance to the class.
3. Invite a parent or friend who does tap dancing, ballet, square dancing, waltz, or polka to demonstrate a few steps for the class.

1st week NATIONAL HUMOR WEEK
Celebrate by:
1. National Humor Week is celebrated to recognize how humor can improve our health and enrich our lives. What is the funniest cartoon character? Have older children imitate their "funny character" and have the rest of the class guess whom the student is imitating.
2. Have small groups choose one of the following: read a funny comic strip, tell a funny joke, present a funny skit, or sing a funny song for the class.
3. Make a "laugh track" by having students trace around their shoes and cut out the pattern. On the cut-out write "laugh words" such as tee hee, ha ha, ho ho, haw haw. Tape the words to make tracks around the room. Throughout the week, have students take turns reading "around the track."
4. Start with the first student and have him or her say, "ha." Go around the room having each student increase the number of "has" (this usually brings on laughter). After the last person has participated, ask why this activity was humorous.

1st week NATIONAL READ-A-ROAD MAP WEEK
Celebrate by:
1. Check with your Automobile Club or Chamber of Commerce for road maps of your state for each student. Explain the maps, such as how to find miles between cities, designation of roads (freeways, turnpikes, surface roads) and the direction of state and national road systems. Note symbols for national parks, the capital and national monuments.
2. Instruct students to find: the capital or another city; which highways go into the city; which road crosses a certain river, and so on.
3. Work in small groups and plot a trip across the state, east to west or north to south. List the starting point, destination, cities passed through, and the roads traveled.

2nd week NATIONAL GARDEN WEEK
   See: National Garden Month, April.

1st week after Easter EGG SALAD WEEK
Celebrate by:
   See: National Egg Month, May; Champion Egg Layer, September 11.
1. Compare an egg broken in a bowl to one hard-boiled and peeled. Cut the cooked egg in half lengthwise and again compare with the one in the bowl.
2. Hard-boil enough eggs to make egg salad for the class. Have students work in small groups to mash the eggs and add enough sandwich spread so the mixture can be spread on a half - slice of bread for an open-face sandwich (one egg should serve four).

2nd week NATIONAL LIBRARY WEEK
Celebrate by:
1. Assign small groups to interview a librarian from a school, university or textbook library
2. Make a graph, using small paper book shapes, to document the students who have, and those who do not have public library cards.

3rd week NATIONAL COIN WEEK
Celebrate by:
1. Coin collectors are often called numismatists (from the Greek words meaning a piece of money). Bring sets of coins in each denomination. Place them in plastic coin sheets (available at coin or hobby shops). Pass them out to small groups. Have them examine the coins, front and back, and discuss them.
2. Have them locate the mint date; the place where minted (no mark is Philadelphia, a small "d" is Denver, and an "s" is for San Francisco). Locate these cities on the map. Older students may be able to identify the metal used in each coin.
3. To test observation skills, collect the coins. Have students write down the six denominations, then the name of the person whose picture appears on each coin.
4. Encourage students to start a collection of pennies and have a "penny swap" day for them to trade coins to add to their collections.

3rd week NATIONAL PET ID WEEK
Celebrate by:
1. Discuss how dogs and cats can be identified.
2. Find out how butterflies, birds, dairy cows, and zoo animals are tagged for identification.
3. If your pet did not have a license, what are some ways you could identify it?

3rd week NATIONAL WEEK OF THE OCEAN
Celebrate by:
1. On a map, locate the nearest ocean. What is its name?
2. List the animals from your ocean that are sources for food. How many of these animals have you eaten?

3rd week READING IS FUN WEEK
Celebrate by:
1. Set aside a special time each day during this week for silent "fun" reading.
2. Arrange for your students to read to a younger class on a one to one basis.
3. Suggest to your students that during this week they offer to read to shut-ins, younger children, neighbors, or to their families.

3rd week **NATIONAL VOLUNTEER WEEK**
Celebrate by:
1. Discuss ways students can volunteer in class, at school, at home, and in their church community.
2. Give each student an "I Will Volunteer" sheet (page 72) to complete.

3rd week **WEEK OF THE YOUNG CHILD**
Celebrate by:
1. Have students make a picture, card or toy (such as a sock toy) to share with a preschool or kindergarten child.
2. Have students make popcorn or trail mix bags to share with a nursery school. Make arrangements ahead of time and ask for a list of names so names and a card can be attached to the bags. Have a parent deliver the gift bags and tell who sent them and why.
3. Arrange to visit a preschool or kindergarten. Have students pair off with a youngster and be a "buddy" for an hour—playing a game, reading to a child, or doing an art activity.
4. Have each student interview a preschool, nursery school or kindergarten teacher.

4th week **NATIONAL SCIENCE AND TECHNOLOGY WEEK**
Celebrate by:
1. This day is celebrated to promote awareness of science and technology, especially among children. Have two students look up the meaning of these two words.
2. Have students predict how much water a cup filled with ice will contain after the ice has melted. Test and find out.
3. Give each student a straw and half cup of water. Go outside and then add one tablespoon of liquid soap to the cup. Blow bubbles for several minutes. Do research to find out about surface tension—what holds the bubbles together and what makes them pop.
4. Examine the tips of fingers, a strand of hair, a piece of lead from a pencil, or other objects with a magnifying glass. Experiment with binoculars, magnets and a microscope.

4th week **NATIONAL BUBBLE GUM WEEK**
Celebrate by:
1. Review what the class discovered about the soap bubbles they blew. Give each student a piece of bubble gum and allow a few minutes for blowing bubbles. Compare the two types of bubbles—soap and gum.
2. Research the origin and history of bubble gum.
3. Ask students who collect bubble gum cards to bring in a few to show the class. Note the different varieties and who manufactures them. Discuss why companies include "cards" in bubble gum packages.

EASTER

Palm Sunday is always the first Sunday before Easter Sunday. Most Christians celebrate Easter on a Sunday between March 22 and April 25—no earlier, no later. Easter falls on the first Sunday after the first full moon on or after March 21. Good Friday is always the Friday before Easter Sunday.

Easter falls on one of the following dates:

1994   April 3
1995   April 16
1996   April 7
1997   March 30
1998   April 12
1999   April 4
2000   April 23

Celebrate by:

1. Have small groups research to find the origin of one of the Easter symbols—egg, lamb, rabbit, chicken, basket.
2. Look into Easter customs celebrated in other countries or among other cultures.
3. Contact someone in your community (or find a book in the library on Ukrainian egg painting), to share Ukrainian painted eggs and give a demonstration. Have students experiment with this art form.
4. Give each student a copy of "Jointed Rabbit" (page 71) to complete. Suggest that they might like to give them to younger children as Easter gifts.

1st Sunday DAYLIGHT SAVINGS TIME

Celebrate by:

1. The first Daylight Savings Time went into effect Easter Sunday, March 31, 1918. A Congressional Act amended it in 1986 to go into effect on the first Sunday of April at 2 a.m. Find out why it was started and why it was amended.
2. A rule to help you remember how to adjust your clock is: Spring forward and fall back. Count the clocks and watches in your household to see how many you will need to move forward an hour.

1 APRIL FOOL'S DAY

Celebrate by:

1. This day is also called All Fool's Day. Tell the class how the farmers in the South harvest the spaghetti fields each spring. Stretch the story out until the students catch on and then add, "Happy April Fool's Day!"
2. Write the words, "court jester" on the chalkboard and ask students who they think this person was and the nature of the court jester's job. Explain that a court jester (fool) entertained royal or noble families and dressed in colorful costumes and performed tricks and skits. Write a story about the day you were a court jester.

2 HANS CHRISTIAN ANDERSEN'S BIRTHDAY (1805–1875)

Celebrate by:

1. Find out what students know about this man. Write these facts on a classroom chart. Ask if they knew he was born in Denmark and was a sad and lonely man. Have each student find out five additional things about Hans Christian Andersen. Add them to the chart.
2. "The Ugly Duckling" is said to be a story of the author's life. Based on the information collected by the students, discuss the similarities found in Hans Christian Andersen's life and this fairy tale.
3. Have students each bring in one of Andersen's fairy tale books. Allow time for students to look through and read some of the fairy tales.

2 INTERNATIONAL CHILDREN'S BOOK DAY

Celebrate by:

1. This day is generally celebrated in conjunction with Hans Christian Andersen's birthday. Bring in books about different cultures for students to read and discuss.
2. Invite a parent or family member to read a book or story based on another culture.
3. Invite a local storyteller to come in and tell an oral story to the class, or prepare and tell a story yourself.

2 UNITED STATES MINT ANNIVERSARY (1792)

Celebrate by:

1. *See:* 3rd week of April, National Coin Week. The first mint was established in the United States in 1792. Find out in which city it was located; where later mints were located; if they are still minting coins; and about the Gold Depository at Fort Knox, Kentucky.

3 PONY EXPRESS SERVICE BEGINS (1860)

Celebrate by:

1. Ask for input on what students know about the Pony Express.
2. Provide students with copies of "All In A Day's Ride" (page 73) to complete.
3. Write a letter (or more than one) to the class. Place it in a sealed envelope. Set up a "letter-carrying people express relay." At the end of the relay, open and read the letter.

5 BOOKER T. WASHINGTON'S BIRTHDAY (1856–1915)
Celebrate by:
1. Washington's middle name was Taliaffero and he was born a slave in Hales Ford, Virginia (near Roanoke). Locate his birthplace. Have students give their middle names, tell where they were born, and point out the state or country on a map.
2. Give the students a choice: Booker T. Washington was the inventor of the maple syrup basket; first African American to graduate from college; made 118 products from sweet potatoes; was the first African American to have his name on a United States stamp. Tally the answers. Correct answer: First African American to have his picture on a United States postage stamp (1940).

6 NORTH POLE DISCOVERED (1909)
Celebrate by:
1. *See:* December 14, South Pole Discovered. What is the North Pole? Locate it on the map. Find out who discovered it and what was found there.
2. Experiment with a compass. Can you make the needle point a direction other than north? (No, the compass needle always points north, toward the North Magnetic Pole.)

12 ANNIVERSARY OF THE BIG WIND
Celebrate by:
1. The highest natural wind speed ever recorded was on this date in 1934 at Mount Washington, New Hampshire. Gusts of wind reached 231 miles per hour. Check with your local weather, radio or TV station for the highest wind speed ever recorded in your city.
2. Check the local newspaper and record the daily wind velocity (speed) over a week's period.
3. Discuss the cause of wind, its harmful effects and its benefits.

14 FIRST MCDONALD'S OPENS
Celebrate by:
1. The first McDonald's restaurant opened on this date in 1955. Find out how many McDonald's restaurants there are in your city, the closest one to your school, and how far away it is. Discuss what would be the easiest and quickest way to find this information (Yellow Pages).
2. If one McDonald's sells 1,000 hamburgers each day, find out how many it would sell in a week if it were open everyday, and how many in a month.
3. Discuss from which animal hamburger comes, and how it is made. Take a vote to see what students would order at McDonald's if they could have any item of their choice. Tally the answers and have each student make a picture graph to show the results of the voting.
4. From construction paper, have students cut two circles to represent hamburger buns. Have them cut out additional shapes to show what they like on their favorite hamburgers. Make the sandwiches.

14 FIRST WEBSTER DICTIONARY COMPILED (1806)
See: October 16, Noah Webster's Birthday.

15 INCOME TAX PAYDAY
Celebrate by:
1. Everyone in the United States who makes over a certain amount of money during the year must pay federal and state taxes. This is the date taxes are due. Have students list some of the things they think tax money pays for at the state and the federal levels.
2. Pick up a tax form for each student. Read over the forms and discuss how to fill them out. With older students, let them fill in an imaginary income.
3. Give examples such as if you made $50,000 in a year and paid 10% in taxes, how much would you have left to spend? Younger students—If you made $10.00 and had to pay $1.00 for every ten dollars you made, how much money would you have left?

15 RUBBER ERASER DAY
Celebrate by:
1. Count the number of pencils belonging to the students, that have erasers. Count the number of separate erasers. Make a graph to show the number of each.
2. Graph the class erasers by color.
3. At the beginning of a day, instruct students to put away all their pencils and erasers and not use them for the entire day. Then give them each a small pencil without an eraser to use. At the end of the day, discuss the importance of an eraser.

3rd Friday NATIONAL WHISTLERS' DAY
Celebrate by:
1. An annual three-day event (Friday through Sunday) held in Louisburg, North Carolina, and other areas of the country. Have everyone whistle at once for a few seconds. Discuss how we whistle and what makes the sound.
2. Ask students to bring in any whistles they may have. Compare the similarities and differences of the whistles and of the sounds they make.
3. Divide the class into groups. Have each group practice whistling a well-known tune of their choice. Then whistle the tune for the class to guess the name of the song.
4. Give each student a cracker. When you say "go" they are to eat the crackers and then whistle. Discuss why it was difficult to whistle.

16 WILBUR WRIGHT'S BIRTHDAY (1867–1912)
Celebrate by:
1. *See:* August 19, Orville Wright's birthday; December 17, Wright Brothers' First Powered Flight. Wilbur was born in Millville, Indiana. Find Indiana on the map. The Wright brothers' first powered flight was in 1903. How old was Wilbur when they made the flight? How old was he when he died?
2. Assign students to check with an airport or with a pilot and find out how fast different kinds of planes fly today, such as private, commercial and military planes.
3. Check with a hobby shop to see if there is anyone in your community who would be willing to come to school and give a demonstration of a powered model airplane.

20 NATIONAL LOOK-A-LIKE DAY

Celebrate by:

1. Did anyone ever tell you that you looked like someone famous? Who would you most like to look like?
2. Working in pairs, have students plan how they will make themselves into look-a-likes (create masks, hair styles, make up, wardrobes—including hats, gloves, and shoes).
3. On the designated day, have a special time to celebrate the look-a-likes. See if the class can guess who each pair looks like! Take photographs of each pair or of the class and post in the classroom.

21 KINDERGARTEN DAY

Celebrate by:

1. Kindergarten Day is observed on the anniversary of the birth of Friedrick Froebel (1782–1852), a German educator who started the first kindergarten in 1837. The name means kinder = children and garten = garden, or a garden for children. Compare kindergarten to first grade.
2. Have each student write an essay on why he or she thinks kindergarten is important.

21 QUEEN ELIZABETH'S BIRTHDAY (1926–   )

Celebrate by:

1. Queen Elizabeth II is the Queen of England. Find England on the map. Give each student a copy of "I Went to London to Visit the Queen" (page 74) to complete.
2. If you were the Queen or King of England, how would you like to celebrate your birthday?

22 EARTH DAY

Celebrate by:

1. Earth Day was first observed on this day in 1970 with the message "Give Earth A Chance." Discuss with students why they think this is an important day to celebrate or observe.
2. Have students write pledges to themselves stating what they will try to do for our planet to observe Earth Day.
3. Plan a class project to collect and recycle material that can be sold such as aluminum cans or glass bottles. Decide how you will use the profits in celebration of Earth Day.

23 WILLIAM SHAKESPEARE'S BIRTHDAY (1564–1616)

Celebrate by:

1. William Shakespeare, an English poet and playwright, died on his birth date in 1616. How old was he? Find out if any students have read, had read to, or seen his plays.
2. Read a few lines of some of his works to the class. Have students take turns reading a few lines "with great feeling and emotion."
3. How long has it been since Shakespeare died? Why do you think his books and plays are still popular today?

26 JOHN AUDUBON (1785–1851)

Celebrate by:

1. John Audubon, an American artist and naturalist, was born in Haiti. Find Haiti on the map.
2. He was an ornithologist. What do you think this term means? He was one of the first Americans to study and paint birds.
3. Research your favorite bird.
4. Paint a picture of your favorite bird. Check with a librarian to see if you can find any copies of bird paintings by John Audubon to share with the class.

27 SECRETARY'S DAY

Celebrate by:

1. Ask students if they know someone who is a secretary. Discuss the duties of a secretary.
2. Check to see if there is a parent who is a secretary who would come to class and share about this career.
3. Arrange a visit to the school secretary's office and have him or her give the students an overview of the duties of a secretary, explain the business machines used, demonstrate shorthand and how to take notes.

28 MARYLAND ADMISSION DAY

Celebrate by:

1. Maryland became the 7th state in 1788. Add this information to your United States Map (page 13). Lightly color the state with crayon or colored pencil.
2. Write this state opposite its number on the State Admission Order page (page 15).

30 LOUISIANA ADMISSION DAY

Celebrate by:

1. Louisiana became the 18th state in 1812. Add this information to your United States Map (page 13). Lightly color the state with crayon or colored pencil.
2. Write this state opposite its number on the State Admission Order page (page 15).

Last Friday NATIONAL ARBOR DAY (PROPOSED)

Celebrate by:

1. Arbor Day—when is it? This is a difficult question as it varies from state to state and sometimes within counties. It is celebrated by Nebraska in April, in some southern states and Hawaii in either December or March, in parts of Arizona in February, and in some counties in April. When is it celebrated in your state or city?
2. Find out: when was the first Arbor Day; where and why was it held; of whom is the day in honor; when was the date changed? April 30 is the day being proposed as National Arbor Day.
3. Find out the name of your state tree. Try to arrange to purchase (or have donated) a small state tree and plant it in your school yard.
4. Discuss the possibility of planting a flowering tree at a nursing home, facility for the handicapped or other local facility.

JOINTED RABBIT

Color or decorate the rabbit parts. Cut out the rabbit parts. Glue a cottonball on for a tail. Fasten together by pushing a paper fastener through the marked holes.

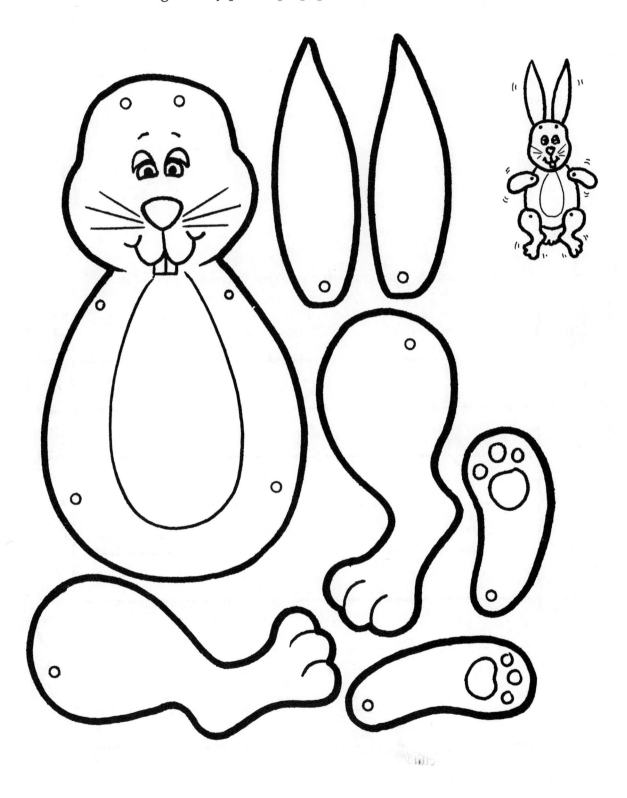

3rd Week in April – NATIONAL VOLUNTEER WEEK

I WILL VOLUNTEER

Opposite each location, list your volunteer jobs.
Write in the date you complete your volunteer projects.

Location	Volunteer Project	Date Completed
Home		
School		
Community		

Write a paragraph about which project you enjoyed the most.

_____

_____

_____

_____

_____

_____

_____

_____

April 3 – PONY EXPRESS SERVICE BEGINS

ALL IN A DAY'S RIDE

The Pony Express service began in 1860. It was a system of delivering mail from St. Joseph, Missouri to Sacramento, California. It followed a trail from Missouri to Nebraska, to Wyoming, to Utah, to Nevada, and then to California.

1. Draw a line from St. Joseph through each of these states into Sacramento.
2. Draw a rider on the running horse.
3. Draw a fence around the standing horses.
4. The Pony Express began on April 3, 1860 and ended on October 24, 1861. For how many months was the mail carried by the Pony Express?

The mail was placed in pouches and carried by riders on fast horses. They worked in relays and switched horses at each relay station. The relay stations were about every 10 miles along the route. The distance between the two cities was about 2,000 miles. By using the relay system, the riders could cover the distance in about 10 days.

5. How many miles did the riders cover in one day?

April 21 – QUEEN ELIZABETH'S BIRTHDAY

I WENT TO LONDON TO VISIT THE QUEEN

Fill in the blanks. Draw faces for each person in the empty spaces.

Elizabeth Alexandra Mary   is the Queen of England.

She was born in 1926 and is now _____ years old.

Her husband is Prince Philip   . They have four children—

Prince Charles   , Princess Anne   ,

Prince Andrew   , and Prince Edward   .

Her mother is Queen Elizabeth, the Queen Mother   .

She was born in 1900. She is now _____ years old.

The Queen lives in a castle.

Draw a picture of a castle.

May

Flower – Hawthorn and lily of the valley
Birthstone – Emerald

May is the fifth month of the year. Although it was the third month on the early Roman calendar, it has always had thirty-one days. Thoughts of May usually include May flowers, bird nests, flowering trees, and green grass.

MONTH

AMERICAN BIKE MONTH
Celebrate by:
1. Survey the kinds and colors of bikes owned by students or family members. Graph the results.
2. Discuss bicycle safety.
3. Arrange with the local police or a bike shop to set up a "bicycle safety check."

CORRECT POSTURE MONTH
Celebrate by:
1. Ask what students think is "good" posture and what is "poor" posture. Demonstrate good posture for students such as stomach in, hips under, chest out, shoulders back, and head erect.
2. Discuss why good posture is important to practice. Encourage students to compliment each other when they notice good posture practices.

NATIONAL ALLERGY/ASTHMA MONTH
Celebrate by:
1. Discuss the symptoms of allergies, asthma and hay fever (all three are common chronic ailments among children).
2. Discuss some of the causes of the three ailments (house dust, pollen and food).
3. Invite an allergist to speak to the students on ways to recognize, avoid, and control asthma, allergies, and hay fever.

NATIONAL EGG MONTH
Celebrate by:
1. *See:* April, Egg Salad Week. How many ways can students think of to serve eggs?
2. Separate the white and the yolk from an egg into two bowls. Explain the parts of an egg. Observe and describe the contents of the two bowls. Beat each separately with a hand rotary egg beater (or fork or wire whisk). Note, describe, and discuss students' observations.
3. Give each student a copy of "The Egg and I" (page 88) to complete.

NATIONAL HIGH BLOOD PRESSURE MONTH

Celebrate by:

1. Assign four students to look up the following terms and write the definitions on the chalk board: blood pressure, systolic, diastolic, and pulse. Discuss these terms. Have students locate the pulse in their wrists.
2. Obtain a home blood pressure kit (some families may have one you can borrow). Demonstrate its use. Have another adult supervise while students take their own blood pressures and record them.
3. Explain how to take one's pulse. Have students take and record their pulse rates. Assign a student to look up the normal blood pressure and another to locate the average pulse rate. Write these numbers on the chalkboard so students can make a comparison.

NATIONAL PHYSICAL FITNESS MONTH

Celebrate by:

1. Discuss ways students can stay physically fit.
2. Have students work in small groups to come up with an exercise or physical fitness activity and be prepared to explain how it aids in physical fitness. Review each group's contribution.
3. Take time each day throughout this month to do the activities planned by the students.

NATIONAL SALAD MONTH

Celebrate by:

1. Lettuce is the main ingredient in the majority of salads. Ask students to name different kinds of lettuce. Provide as many types as possible for students to examine. Discuss similarities and differences in the lettuce varieties.
2. Wash the lettuce and do a taste test comparison.
3. Use the remaining lettuce to make a salad. Ask students to each bring in a vegetable to add to the salad. Provide salad dressing, bowls, safe cutting knives, and forks. Have each student make his or her own salad stating they must include a piece of each vegetable.
4. Discuss other types of salads such as fruit, meat, and frozen salads.

WEEK

1st week BE KIND TO ANIMALS' WEEK

Celebrate by:

1. *See:* April, Prevent Animal Cruelty Month. Declare a special "dog day" in your classroom. Have students make a list of professionals who provide services or different uses of dogs (veterinarian, dog groomer or boarder, seeing-eye, police, or show dog).
2. Have students bring in photographs of their dog or cat, or a picture cut from a magazine to post on the bulletin board. Let each student be responsible for telling about his or her breed of animal.

1st week **NATIONAL FAMILY WEEK**

Celebrate by:

1. *See:* August 8, American Family Day. Have students share things they and their families enjoy doing together.
2. Have each student write about a special trip, outing, or visit he or she has had with a member of his or her immediate or extended family.
3. Have each student plan an activity or outing for his or her family. Encourage the students to talk their ideas over with their families, and if family members are agreeable, be responsible for carrying out the plans.

1st week **NATIONAL HERB WEEK**

Celebrate by:

1. Bring samples of herbs. Have students learn to identify and spell the names of each.
2. Assign a small group an herb to research and decide ways it can be used.
3. Decide on a few herbs students would like to grow. Provide seeds and pots or a window box, or plant them outdoors. Have students make a work chart so each takes a turn carrying for their garden.

1st week **NATIONAL PET WEEK**

Celebrate by:

1. Debate the issue of which makes the better pet—a dog or a cat. Divide the class into two groups: the cats and the dogs. Have each student decide how his or her assigned animal makes the better pet and prepare a statement. Allow each student one minute to present his or her part of the debate.
2. Find out who has the most unusual pet. What is the most unusual pet you have ever encountered?

1st week **NATIONAL POSTCARD WEEK**

Celebrate by:

1. Have students bring in picture postcards postmarked in different cities, states or countries. Share with the class the place from which your card was sent. Point out the location on a map.
2. Picture postcards often show a museum, historical location or other visitor attraction. Discuss the pictures on the cards students brought.
3. Provide unruled 4" x 6" white cards. Have students make their own picture postcards and rule one side for a message and address.
4. Show and discuss a United States Postal card. Note the "stamp." The first United States Postal cards sold for one-cent and were called penny postcards. Note the amount of postage due when sending a postcard. How much more does it cost to send a letter than a postcard?

1st week **NATIONAL RAISIN WEEK**

Celebrate by:

1. Ask students if they know from where raisins come. Taste a black and a white raisin. Compare the two tastes.
2. Soak raisins in warm water. Discuss the students' observations. What science concept took place in the experiment? (absorption)
3. Plan to make raisin cookies, tarts or pudding. Ask students to help find a recipe, and make a list of the ingredients needed to make a serving for each member of the class.

1st week NATIONAL TOURISM WEEK
Celebrate by:
1. Have each student make a list of places in or near your city that they think tourists would enjoy visiting.
2. Ask travel agencies for out-dated travel literature. Have students look through the brochures and decide on a place they would like to visit. Have students write essays telling why they would like to visit this place and what they might expect to see there.

2nd week NATIONAL HOSPITAL WEEK
Celebrate by:
1. Make arrangements to tour a hospital. Ask permission for your class to sing a song to the patients.
2. Inquire if students have been patients in a hospital. Discuss experiences such as meals, visitors, doctor visits, and medication.
3. Discuss different kinds of hospitals of which students are aware.

2nd week NATIONAL POLICE WEEK
Celebrate by:
1. National Police Week was established in 1963. Discuss the similarities and differences among the three law enforcement agencies—local police, highway patrol, and sheriff departments.
2. Make a list of ways you, as a good citizen, can help your local police department.

2nd week NATIONAL NURSING HOME WEEK
Celebrate by:
1. Have students find out about the nursing homes in your area. Make a classroom list.
2. Decide on a nursing home your class would like to adopt for the week. Let students make plans for what they will do for their adopted group.

2nd week NATIONAL SALVATION ARMY WEEK
   See: March 10, Salvation Army.

DAY

1 ASTRONOMY DAY
Celebrate by:
1. The first planetarium in the United States opened in Chicago, Illinois, in 1930. What is a planetarium and what is its purpose?
2. If there is a planetarium nearby, arrange a visit, or invite one of the scientists to visit your class.
3. Have someone come and demonstrate a telescope.
4. Encourage students to look and study the stars for several nights, and record their observations to share with the class.

1 FIRST SKYSCRAPER

Celebrate by:

1. The first skyscraper, The Home Insurance Building, was built in Chicago in 1884. The building was ten stories high. It was torn down in 1931. Have each student find out the tallest building in your city and its height. Research and record four other skyscrapers, include the date of construction, and the height.
2. Have students use their research information to make a time line for their five buildings, showing the height (either by feet or stories) and the date of construction for each.
3. If any students have visited the Empire State Building or other skyscrapers, ask them to share photographs, postcards and souvenirs.

1 LEI DAY

Celebrate by:

1. Celebrate this special Hawaiian day by making leis from fresh, plastic, paper, or egg-cup (from egg cartons) flowers. String the flowers and wear the lei around your neck. Flower leis can also be made to wear around the ankle or wrist.
2. Locate a parent or someone in the community to come to class and teach a simple hula.
3. Listen to Hawaiian music and learn a short song.
4. Ask parents to provide toothpicks, pineapple and other fresh fruits for students to prepare and serve on toothpicks. Have a lei party—wear leis, sing, dance, and eat!

1 MAY DAY

Celebrate by:

1. Find out about the custom of giving May baskets. Discuss ways in which students could make baskets and what material in the classroom is available for use. Have each student design and make a May basket to give away. Ask parents to provide flowers.
2. Assign small groups to find out how another country or culture celebrates May Day. Lei Day is the Hawaiian version of May Day.

1 MOTHER GOOSE DAY

Celebrate by:

1. Who was Mother Goose? Legend has it that Mother Goose was actually several different people. Have students see what they can find out about this legendary character.
2. Bring in a collection of Mother Goose rhymes. Have students take turns reading them.
3. Select a short nursery rhyme to write on the chalkboard. Have students write another verse to the rhyme.
4. Write familiar nursery rhymes on 3" x 5" cards. Divide the class into groups. Give each group a card. Assign a time limit for deciding how the group will dramatize the rhyme. Present to the class.
5. Have students draw pictures of how they think Mother Goose really appeared.

4 NATIONAL TEACHER'S DAY

Celebrate by:

1. Discuss how we could honor one of our teachers such as the art, music or reading specialist.
2. Make cards or pictures. Bring flowers to arrange in a decorated jar or can.
3. Create a song, skit or poem about a special teacher.
4. Invite one or more teachers to class to be honored with songs, cards and flowers.

4 NATIONAL WEATHER OBSERVER'S DAY
Celebrate by:
1. Have each student record the high and low temperatures and the cloud cover for the day.
2. Check a resource book to research the different kinds of clouds and how they appear.
3. Have students predict the high and low temperatures and the cloud cover for the next few days. Bring in a newspaper each morning and have them check their predictions against the actual weather conditions.

5 FIRST AMERICAN IN SPACE
Celebrate by:
1. Who was the first American in space? Who was the first man in space?
2. Our first space ship reached a speed of 500 miles an hour. Find out how fast your family car will go. How much faster did our first space ship travel than your family car? What is the speed limit on most highways?
3. Discuss whether students think it is important to explore space and why.

5 JAPAN CHILDREN'S DAY
Celebrate by:
1. Japan Children's Day is always celebrated on the fifth day of the fifth month. Fish kites are a popular way of observing this day. Precut two large fish (or provide a pattern) for students to glue together around the edges, leaving the mouth open. Decorate the fish and punch a hole in the side of the open end. Attach a long string, and run into the wind with the kite. A carp is the fish the kite usually depicts, and it is usually painted in red and orange colors.
2. Have students see what else they can discover about this special day in Japan.
3. Find out if there is a parent or community member who would come and demonstrate a traditional Japanese tea or other cultural custom.

5 CINCO DE MAYO DAY
Celebrate by:
1. Find out if anyone is from Mexico or has been a visitor there. Ask them to share the reason for this special day and different ways it is celebrated.
2. Make a large piñata or have older students each make a small one. Check books in the library on how to make a piñata or inquire of a parent or community member.
3. Listen to Mexican music and learn a Mexican dance.

5 NATIONAL HOAGIE DAY
Celebrate by:
1. This day is in honor of the city of Philadelphia, Pennsylvania's official sandwich. Find out if your city has an official sandwich. If not, have students write essays telling what they think it should be and why.
2. Provide a large loaf of French bread and ingredients for students to make a giant hoagie sandwich.
3. Write a class letter asking what ingredients are in the Philadelphia giant hoagie. Send it to Wawa, Inc., Baltimore Pike, Wawa, PA 19063.

1st Thursday NATIONAL DAY OF PRAYER
Celebrate by:
1. This day in 1981, a Presidential Proclamation was issued declaring a National Day of Prayer. Find out how your city and local churches observe this day.
2. Find out at which hour your city or a larger nearby city observes this day. At the designated time, allow one minute for silent prayer or "good thoughts" about others, our nation and the world.

1st Friday and Saturday ARMADILLO FESTIVAL
Celebrate by:
1. The Armadillo Festival is held each year in Hamburg, Arkansas. Draw a picture of an armadillo.
2. Check a resource book to see how accurate your drawing is. Where in the United States is this animal found?
3. Use clay to create an armadillo.

8 NO SOCKS DAY
Celebrate by:
1. Using a complete sentence, use three adjectives to describe your socks.
2. If no one in our class wore socks today, how many pairs of socks would that save from laundering? Find out the number of students in your school. If no one wore socks to school for a day (or week), how many pairs of socks would that save from laundering? How would these "no socks" days aid the environment?
3. Tomorrow wear your favorite socks. Be prepared to tell why they are your favorite and from what kind of material your socks are made.

8 V-E DAY
Celebrate by:
1. Provide each student with a copy of "Victory Day" (page 89) to complete.
2. Using the list of countries from "Victory Day," locate each one on a map. Then find the capital of each country.

8 WORLD RED CROSS DAY
Celebrate by:
1. *See:* December 24, Clara Barton's Birthday. The Red Cross was founded in Switzerland in 1863 by Jean Henry Dunant. Find this country on a map.
2. Bring in pictures from magazines and newspapers about the Red Cross and display them on the bulletin board.
3. Cut large red crosses from construction paper. On each cross, write one service of the Red Cross. Post the crosses around the room.
4. What is the Geneva Convention and what does it have to do with the Red Cross?

9 SIR JAMES BARRIE'S BIRTHDAY (1860–1937)

Celebrate by:

1. Find out if anyone knows who this man was and why we honor him with a special day. If not, have them find out.
2. Barrie was a Scottish playwright and novelist who is best known for his play, book, and the eventual Disney film of Peter Pan. Bring in the story and have each student take turns reading a few lines.
3. Peter Pan was a little boy who never grew older. Draw a picture of yourself in Never-Never Land.

11 MINNESOTA ADMISSION DAY

Celebrate by:

1. Minnesota became the 32nd state in 1858. Add this information to your United States map (page 13). Color the state lightly with colored pencil or crayon.
2. Write this state opposite its number on the State Admission Order page (page 15).

2nd Sunday MOTHER'S DAY

Celebrate by:

1. Mother's Day was first observed in 1907. Find out how it originated.
2. Have each student cut a small picture of himself or herself to fit inside a jar lid, then glue a small refrigerator magnet on the back. Finally, the student can make and decorate an envelope or bag to hold his or her gift and give it to his or her mother or another family member.
3. Have each student make a card and list inside three things he or she does not usually do, but will do without being told over the next few days.
4. At the end of the week, have students share their mom's reaction to the "gift list" cards.

12 LIMERICK DAY

Celebrate by:

1. Read several limericks from Edward Leer's (the man who made this form popular) *A Book of Nonsense* to the class. Discuss length, rhyme, rhythm, and beginning and end of typical limericks.
2. Have each student write a limerick and read it to the class.
3. If you have a computer in the classroom, have each student enter his or her limerick (discuss format first). Print out copies for each student.

12 FLORENCE NIGHTINGALE'S BIRTHDAY

Celebrate by:

1. Florence Nightingale was a nurse and a public health activist who promoted nursing as a profession. Find out how she did this.
2. Interview a nurse. Find out about his or her job, educational requirements, duties, hours he or she works, and how long he or she has been a nurse.
3. Have students write a paragraph about why they would or would not like to be a nurse.

2nd weekend CALAVERAS COUNTY FROG JUMPING JUBILEE

Celebrate by:

1. This annual four-day event, held in Calaveras County, California, brings in over 3,000 frogs from around the world. Find out what Mark Twain has to do with this event. (*See:* November 30, Samuel Clemens' Birthday.)
2. Divide the class into three groups to research a frog, toad and bull frog. After each group reports to the class, compare the three.
3. Discuss the metamorphosis a frog undergoes.
4. Have a "people frog jumping" contest. Have students start with hands and feet on the ground and jump, landing each time on hands and feet. Jump between boundaries.

14 GABRIEL DANIEL FAHRENHEIT'S BIRTHDAY (1686–1736)

Celebrate by:

1. Write this man's name on the chalkboard and see if anyone can figure out why we would recognize his birthday as a special day.
2. He was a German physicist who developed the Fahrenheit temperature scale. He determined that there were three fixed temperatures: 0 degrees for the freezing point of salt, ice and water mixed together; 32 degrees for the freezing point of pure water; and 96 degrees (he later proved it was 98.6 degrees) for normal body temperature—or 18, 0, 36 degrees on the Celsius scale. Provide thermometers in both scales, cups, salt, ice cubes, and water for students to check the freezing points.
3. Use the two types of thermometers to check and record both indoor and outdoor temperatures for a few days.

14 THOMAS GAINSBOROUGH'S BIRTHDAY (1727–1788)

Celebrate by:

1. Gainsborough was one of the great British painters. His most famous work was *The Blue Boy*. Ask if students have seen pictures of this painting. Locate one from an art book and discuss it with the students. Draw attention to the use of green and blue colors and the use of a landscape background.
2. Have students paint a landscape background and then use blue as the dominant color for a figure.

3rd Saturday ARMED FORCES DAY

Celebrate by:

1. Armed Forces Day was first celebrated in 1950 and was proclaimed by President Harry Truman. List on a classroom chart the branches of the armed forces.
2. Assign groups to research each branch of the armed forces and the role of women in the armed services.
3. Bring in pictures cut from magazines or newspapers, or family photographs representing the different branches. Arrange the pictures on the bulletin board to form a large collage.
4. If there is a military installation nearby, arrange a visit or encourage students and their families to attend the Saturday open house which most facilities have.

15 DINOSAUR BONES DISCOVERED

Celebrate by:

1. Write the word paleontologist on the chalkboard and ask students for a definition. Assign a student to look up the word in the dictionary and read the definition.
2. Scientists discovered a 225 million year old dinosaur skeleton in 1985. What does the word dinosaur mean? (It is from two Greek words meaning terrible lizard.)
3. Compare pictures of the skeletons of dinosaurs, birds, and lizards.
4. Press shells, chicken bones, leaves, and pieces of bark into a flat piece of clay. Carefully remove the objects and dry the clay in the sun to make your own fossil prints.
5. Dinosaur National Monument was established in 1915. Where is it located? Find the location on the map. (It is on the Utah/Colorado border.)

15 CHARLES LINDBERGH'S TRANSATLANTIC FLIGHT (1927)

See: February 4, Charles Lindbergh's Birthday.

16 BIOGRAPHER'S DAY

Celebrate by:

1. Read a biography of a president, sports figure, inventor, or other person of interest.
2. Explain the difference between biography and autobiography. Have students write their own autobiographies. Include birth, preschool years, and school years up to the present. Add illustrations.

18 INTERNATIONAL MUSEUM DAY

Celebrate by:

1. Discuss things we might see in a museum; how museums are supported; how they benefit us, and the duties of a docent.
2. Visit a museum—art, historical, natural history, Native American.

18 WORLD LARGEST LEGO COMPLETED

Celebrate by:

1. In 1990, the world's largest Lego tower was built. It stood 59.5 feet high. How many yard-sticks would it take to equal the tower's height? Measure the height on the sidewalk.
2. Borrow as many sets of Legos as possible and see how tall a tower your students can build. Take turns working in pairs, a few minutes at a time. Measure the completed tower. How much taller was the record Lego tower?

19 RINGLING BROTHERS FOUNDED THEIR CIRCUS (1884)

Celebrate by:

1. Five American brothers built a small group of performers into the world's largest circus. It opened on this date in Baraboo, Wisconsin. Make a list of performers and acts one might find in a circus.
2. What is the difference between a circus and a carnival?
3. Plan a classroom circus—juggling, tricks, music, acrobats, mime, skits.

21 RED CROSS FOUNDED IN THE UNITED STATES (1881)

See: May 8, World Red Cross Day; December 25, Clara Barton's birthday.

22 ARNOLD LOBEL'S BIRTHDAY (1933–   )

Celebrate by:

1. Read Arnold Lobel's 1981 Caldecott Award book, *Fables.*
2. Bring other fables and have students take turns each reading one. Compare them to Lobel's book.
3. Have students each write a short fable.
4. Find and read other books by Arnold Lobel.

23 SCOTT O'DELL'S BIRTHDAY (1903–   )

Celebrate by:

1. Read and discuss (all or part) of *Island of the Blue Dolphins,* O'Dell's 1961 Newbery Award book.
2. The setting for the story is the Channel Islands which are located off the coast of Southern California. Locate the islands on a map.
3. Find out about the Newbery Award—who gives it, for whom was it named, and for what is it given?

23 SOUTH CAROLINA ADMISSION DAY

Celebrate by:

1. South Carolina became the 8th state in 1788. Add this information to your United States map (page 13). Color the state lightly with colored pencil or crayon.
2. Write this state opposite its number on the State Admission Order page (page 15).

26 and 27 NATIONAL GEOGRAPHY BEE FINALS

Celebrate by:

1. The first place winner from each state Geography Bee competition advances to the national level. Students compete for prizes and scholarships totaling more than $50,000. With the help of the students, organize a geography bee.
2. Have students each submit five to ten questions (and answers) to be used. Select the appropriate ones and add your own for the final "bee." Use the others for a practice "bee."

26 SALLY KRISTEN RIDE'S BIRTHDAY (1951–   )

Celebrate by:

1. Sally Ride was one of the first seven women in the U.S. Astronaut Corps and the first American woman in space. Find out where she was born, whom she married, the name of the space shuttle, where it was launched, where it landed, and the length of the flight.
2. Locate her birthplace, launch site, and landing site on the map.
3. Find out who the first woman in space was and from what country she came. Locate the country on the map.

27 PATENT ON CELLOPHANE TAPE
Celebrate by:
1. List some of the uses for cellophane tape. What do you think people used before it was invented?
2. Provide cellophane tape and drinking straws for students to create a sculpture.

27 RACHEL LOUISE CARSON'S BIRTHDAY (1907–1964)
Celebrate by:
1. Rachel Carson was an American scientist and author. Read and discuss portions of her book, *Silent Spring*, that revealed the harmful effects of pesticides.
2. Pesticides are classified according to the pest they control. Discuss pests. Assign students to look up the words: pesticide, herbicide, insecticide, fungicide.
3. Give students a copy of "Silent Pond" (page 90) to complete.

28 DIONNE QUINTUPLETS' BIRTHDAY
Celebrate by:
1. On this date in 1934, five daughters were born to a couple in Canada, Mr. and Mrs. Dionne. They all lived. They were famous and for many years were the only living quintuplets.
2. Have students ask parents, grandparents or other relatives who might remember this event, to tell them about it and to give them the names of the babies (Marie, Cecile, Yvonne, Emilie, and Annette).
3. The odds of a mother having quintuplets are about one set in 85 million births. What are these multiple birth babies called—two babies; three babies; four babies, six babies?
4. Ask if students know any twins, triplets, or others.

29 RHODE ISLAND ADMISSION DAY
Celebrate by:
1. Rhode Island became the 13th state in 1790. Add this information to your United States map (page 13). Color the state lightly with colored pencil or crayon.
2. Write this state opposite its number on the State Admission Order page (page 15).

29 WISCONSIN ADMISSION DAY
Celebrate by:
1. Wisconsin became the 30th state in 1848. Add this information to your United States map (page 13). Color the state lightly with colored pencil or crayon.
2. Write this state opposite its number on the State Admission Order page (page 15).

30 LINCOLN MEMORIAL DEDICATION
Celebrate by:
1. Give each student a copy of "Mr. Lincoln" (page 91) to complete.
2. Read, or have students read, the Gettysburg Address.

31 MEMORIAL DAY

Celebrate by:

1. Ask for student input regarding this day. This day is also called Decoration Day. Why?
2. Memorial Day was first observed in the United States on May 5, 1865 in Waterloo, New York. It was proclaimed in 1948 to be the last Monday in May as a day of prayer for permanent peace, and it was requested that the flag be flown at half mast.
3. Ask permission to have each student place a flower at the base of the flag pole when the flag is raised.

31 UNITED NATIONAL NO-TOBACCO DAY

Celebrate by:

1. No-Tobacco Day is an observation sponsored by the World Heath Organization. The Great Smoke-Out is observed on the 3rd Thursday of November. Let students share why they feel it is not healthy for a person to smoke, and why it is unhealthy to be around those who smoke.
2. Write a letter to someone you love (like or know) who smokes, telling them why you wish they did not smoke. Mail it!

Month of May—NATIONAL EGG MONTH
THE EGG AND I

Study the picture. Then write the number beside the word it matches.

_____ shell

_____ membrane

_____ air cell

_____ egg white

_____ egg yolk

_____ germ spot

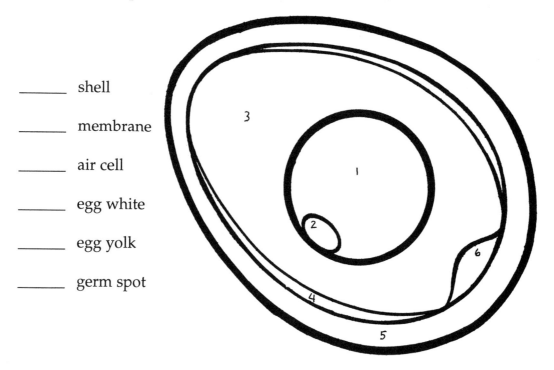

Color the following animals that lay eggs.

birds

chickens

butterflies

turtles

worms

snails

ducks

Name _____

May 8—V-E DAY

VICTORY DAY

V-E Day means Victory in Europe, a day that ended a world war in Europe. Research to find out why this was called "Victory Day."

What was the name of this war?_____

What year did the war begin? _____

What year did this war end? _____

List some of the countries involved in the war. _____

Which countries were fighting against us? _____

Which countries were fighting with us? _____

Who was our president during this war? _____

Ask an older person who lived during this war to tell you about: blackouts, rationing stamps, U.S.O., and air raid drills. Write two sentences about each of these.

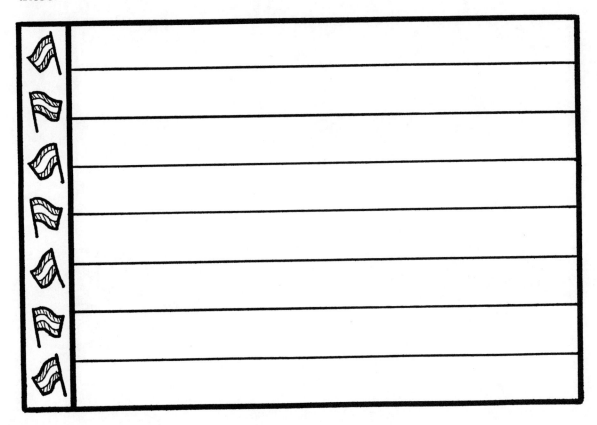

May 27—RACHEL LOUISE CARSON'S BIRTHDAY

SILENT POND

A crop dusting airplane drops pesticides on plants. The plants are eaten by cows, pigs and sheep. The pesticides also seep into the ground and then into lakes and ponds. The animals drink the water. The cows, pigs and sheep are eaten by humans and other animals. This is the food chain.

Draw a picture to show this food chain.

May 30—LINCOLN MEMORIAL DEDICATION

MR. LINCOLN

Find and read information on the Lincoln Memorial. Answer the questions below.

Who sits in the Lincoln memorial?

_____

Where is the Lincoln Memorial located?

_____

What material was used to make the memorial?

_____

How long is the memorial?

_____

How wide is the memorial?

_____

The 36 columns in the memorial stand for

_____

June

Flower – Rose
Birthstone – Pearl, alexandrite, and moonstone

June is the sixth month of the year and contains 31 days. It was the fourth month in the Roman Calendar, and once had only 29 days. The Romans may have named this month after Juno, the goddess of marriage. June is known as the wedding month. Summer begins this month.

MONTH

ADOPT-A-CAT MONTH
Celebrate by:
1. Discuss the care of cats and kittens. Contact the animal shelter or Humane Society and find out how to adopt a cat.
2. Have students check with their families, neighbors, or relatives and explain to them how to adopt a cat.
3. If there is a zoo nearby, check to find out how one can adopt a "big cat." Make a list of animals that belong to the cat family.

DAIRY MONTH
Celebrate by:
1. Dairy Month was established in 1937 as a salute to American dairy producers. Make a class list of dairy products.
2. Bring in pictures of dairy products to exhibit on the bulletin board.
3. Bring in a small picture of a dairy product. Glue it to the top of a sheet of paper. Underneath, write down all the information you can find about this product.

NATIONAL ICE TEA MONTH
Celebrate by:
1. Bring in several boxes of tea, both loose and in bags. Working in small groups, have students read the information on the boxes to find out what kind of tea the box contains, where the tea is from, and how to make ice tea. Discuss countries where tea is grown and locate these places on the map.
2. Smell the tea, discuss caffeinated, decaffeinated, and herbal teas. Decide on the kind to make.
3. To make sun tea, fill quart jars with water, add four tea bags to each jar. Set the jars in the sun for about four hours. Add ice, lemon, honey, and serve.

NATIONAL PAPAYA MONTH

Celebrate by:

1. A month to celebrate the peak season of this fruit from Hawaii. Bring papayas in a paper bag. Have students guess what it is by feeling in the bag, then give clues—grows on a tree in warm, tropical areas such as Hawaii; is shaped like a pear; is ready to eat when it turns yellow.
2. Remove the fruit from the bag and explain what it is. Have students write down their estimates of the number of seeds inside the fruit. Cut, remove seeds, compare with estimates, and dry the seeds for planting later. Taste the fruit.
3. On a small piece of paper, write down one word that describes the taste. Cut out a paper papaya, glue the paper word to it and tape it to the bulletin board.
4. Find out which other states and countries grow papayas. Find these places on a map.

NATIONAL PEST CONTROL MONTH

Celebrate by:

1. Identify household pests, yard pests, and general insects that are considered pests.
2. Assign each student to find (and write down) the meaning of biological control as it relates to pest control. Read these to the class.
3. Discuss how we can help control pests in our neighborhood and around our school.

NATIONAL ROSE MONTH

Celebrate by:

1. Have students bring in cut roses. Examine the parts of the flower, look for similarities and differences—shape, size, texture, aroma, and color among the roses. Make a color graph using tiny roses cut from construction paper.
2. Remove petals from the roses and place in a large pan for a tactile and olfactory experience. Describe the texture and aroma.
3. Spread a piece of wax paper with liquid glue. Arrange rose petals in a design. Top with another piece of wax paper. Press the paper lightly with your hand and then allow it to dry. Punch a hole in the top of the paper and hang it in a sunny window.

WEEK

1st week TEACHER THANK YOU WEEK

Celebrate by:

1. *See:* May 4, National Teacher Day. Have each student make a list of teachers he or she would like to thank. Write the reason for thanking each opposite the name. With younger children, discuss why you might want to thank a teacher and then draw a "thank you" picture.
2. Have students make thank you cards for two or more teachers they would like to thank. They can write their own words or poems and add art work. Older students may also wish to make envelopes for their cards.
3. Ask permission to take your students to the office or teacher's room where mailboxes are located. Let small groups take turns placing their cards in the correct mail spaces.

Week that includes June 14 NATIONAL FLAG WEEK
Celebrate by:
1. *See:* June 14, Flag day; January 1, Betsy Ross' birthday. On April 4, 1818, Congress approved the first flag of the United States. Compare a picture of the first flag to our flag today. Which state is represented by the last star added to our flag? When did this last change take place?
2. Research the origin of the Pledge of Allegiance. Fine out how our Pledge today has changed since the original, and how and why it changed.
3. Read the Pledge of Allegiance slowly to the class and then discuss its meaning.
4. Discuss the care of the flag and when and how to fly or hang it. Encourage students to fly the flag at home on all legal holidays.

2nd week NATIONAL LITTLE LEAGUE BASEBALL WEEK
Celebrate by:
1. Little League was founded in 1939 in Williamsport, Pennsylvania. National Little League Baseball Week was first proclaimed in 1959. It starts on Monday and ends on the following Monday. Girls joined Little League in 1974. Find out how many students play or have played in Little League.
2. Compare Little League with regular baseball—age of players, diamond size, number of innings, uniforms, and shoes.

3rd week NATIONAL CLAY WEEK
Celebrate by:
1. Uhrichsville, Ohio, claims to be the "clay center of the world." Find the state and city on a map (south and east of Canton).
2. Examine clay. Discover of what it consists. If you have clay soil in your area, dig up a bucket and add enough water to make it pliable. Compare it to the classroom clay. Discuss what kind of clay is used for tile, pottery, bricks, and china.
3. Make a sculpture from the class clay and another from the clay dug from the soil. Dry them in the sun and compare them again.
4. Locate a parent or other potter and have him or her come to class and give a demonstration.

DAY

1 KENTUCKY ADMISSION DAY
Celebrate by:
1. Kentucky became the 15th state in 1792. Add this information to your United States map (page 13). Color the state lightly with colored pencil or crayon.
2. Write this state opposite its number on the State Admission Order page (page 15).

1 TENNESSEE ADMISSION DAY
Celebrate by:
1. Tennessee became the 16th state in 1796. Add this information to your United States map (page 13). Color the state lightly with colored pencil or crayon.
2. Write this state opposite its number on the State Admission Order page (page 15).

2 MARTHA WASHINGTON'S BIRTHDAY (1731–1802)

Celebrate by:

1. Martha Dandredge Curtis Washington, the wife of George Washington, was born in New Kent County, Virginia. She became the first First Lady. Compare the present First Lady with the first First Lady.
2. On pieces of paper write the names of presidents so each student has a different name. Have students draw slips of paper and then do research on the wife of the president each drew.

1st Friday DONUT DAY

Celebrate by:

1. Donut Day was founded in 1938 by the Salvation Army as a fundraising event during the Great Depression. Early Dutch settlers brought the "fried cake" to colonial America. Ask a parent who has a doughnut fryer to come to class and help students make doughnuts.
2. Legend suggests a sea captain invented the doughnut hole. Write a humorous paragraph stating why the captain made a hole in the "fried cake."
3. Using the pattern, "Holey Donut Card" (page 99), have students each make a doughnut card and write a "dough-nutty" rhyme or limerick around the hole on the inside of the card.

5 FIRST BALLOON FLIGHT (1903)

Celebrate by:

1. The first hot air balloon flight took place in France in 1783. How many years was this before the Wright Brothers' first airplane flight?
2. Find out if any students have been up in a hot air balloon, or if they have seen a balloon festival. If so, where was it? Ask them to share the experience.

6 D-DAY ANNIVERSARY (1944)

Celebrate by:

1. D-Day is a term for a secret date on which a military operation is to begin. June 6, 1944 is the most famous D-Day. It was the day during World Ward II when British and American troops landed in Normandy, France, which was at the time occupied by Germany. Locate the United States, England, Germany, and France on a map.
2. Look through reference and history books for information on World War II and find out: who was the president of the United States at that time; who led the American troops; who was the leader of Germany at that time?
3. Ask students if someone in their family served in World War II. Invite them to come and speak to the class and share photographs or other mementos. Check with a veteran's organization as they often provide speakers.

9 DONALD DUCK'S BIRTHDAY

Celebrate by:

1. Donald Duck first appeared in 1934 in a short cartoon. What are the names of Donald's uncle and his nephews? Take a vote on the students' favorite—Donald Duck or Mickey Mouse.
2. Read to the class some of the following books about ducks: *The Story About Ping* (Kurt Wiese), *Make Way for Ducklings* (Robert McCloskey's 1942 Caldecott Award book), *Happy Birthday, Dear Duck* (Eve Bunting), *Have You Seen My Duckling?* (Nancy Tafuri).

10 MAURICE SENDAK'S BIRTHDAY (1928–)

Celebrate by:

1. Read Maurice Sendak's book, *Where the Wild Things Are*, to the class. Show the illustrations as you read. Close the book and ask students to tell you about the illustrations.
2. Slowly turn the pages of the book again to show the illustrations. Then ask the question again. Go through the book once more, pointing out the crosshatching (which he uses frequently in his books); how, as the suspense (action) builds, the illustrations grow larger until the pages are filled; the double full pages that appear without any text; how the full page illustrations "bleed" to the edges of the pages; and how the illustrations decrease in size after the climax, as the action and suspense decrease.
3. Make a paper bag puppet to illustrate one of the monsters by decorating the bottom end of the paper bag. Later read the book again and have students use their puppets to act out the action scenes where the monsters play a role.
4. Have students bring in other books that were illustrated, written, or illustrated and written by the author. Note the similarities among the characters in his books. Also look for a dog in each of his books.

14 NATIONAL FLAG DAY

Celebrate by:

1. *See:* January 1, Betsy Ross' Birthday; June 14, National Flag Week. National Flag Day was proclaimed on May 30, 1916 for this date. Discuss the number and location of the stars and stripes on the flag. Have each student make a small paper flag and attach it to a drinking straw.
2. After the morning flag is raised, ask permission for students to parade around the flag pole carrying their flags and singing an appropriate song.
3. Play appropriate music throughout the day and encourage students to sing along at specified times.
4. June 14 at 7:00 p.m. (E.D.T.) is recognized as "Pause for the Pledge," a time for all citizens to share a patriotic moment. Observe your own "pause" sometime during the day.

15 ARKANSAS ADMISSION DAY

Celebrate by:

1. Arkansas became the 25th state in 1836. Add this information to your United States map (page 13). Color the state lightly with colored pencil or crayon.
2. Write this state opposite its number on the State Admission Order page (page 15).

18 FIRST FERRIS WHEEL UNVEILED (1893)

Celebrate by:

1. G.W. Gale Ferris, an engineer, built the largest "pleasure wheel" ever at that time. It was for the Chicago World's Fair. Find Chicago on the map.
2. Discuss experiences your students have had riding Ferris Wheels—when and where, and how it feels when one is at the top of the wheel and it stops.
3. Provide Tinker Toys, Legos, blocks, Erector Sets, or other construction materials for students to build Ferris Wheels.

18 INTERNATIONAL PICNIC DAY

Celebrate by:

1. Plan a class picnic. Decide on the food, how it will be provided, when and where it will be held, and assign tasks to each student or to small groups.
2. Plan a picnic for a younger class. Make arrangements with the teacher. Pair each student with a younger child. Make and send invitations. Hold the picnic on the school premises.

20 BALD EAGLE BECOMES OFFICIAL SYMBOL OF THE UNITED STATES

Celebrate by:

1. This bird became the official symbol of the United States on this day in 1782. Make a list of the places where you can find this symbol.
2. Provide thick paint and give each student a copy of "Double Eagle" (page 100) to complete.
3. Have each student find out five things about the bald eagle. Compile the information and write it on a classroom chart.

20 WEST VIRGINIA ADMISSION DAY

Celebrate by:

1. West Virginia became the 35th state in 1863. Add this information to your United States map (page 13). Color the state lightly with colored pencil or crayon.
2. Write this state opposite its number on the State Admission Order page (page 15).

3rd Sunday FATHER'S DAY

Celebrate by:

1. Father's Day was recognized, but was not presidentially proclaimed until 1966. Find out who first requested this holiday; in which state it was first observed and the dates; and which president made the proclamation.
2. Have students write an essay telling how they would choose to spend Father's Day if they could spend it any way they wished.

21 NEW HAMPSHIRE ADMISSION DAY

Celebrate by:

1. New Hampshire became the 9th state in 1788. Add this information to your United States map (page 13). Color the state lightly with colored pencil or crayon.
2. Write this state opposite its number on the State Admission Order page (page 15).

21 or 22 SUMMER BEGINS

Celebrate by:

1. The summer solstice begins either June 21 or 22 of each year. Which day this year will have the largest amount of daylight hours?
2. Have students choose one day during the first week of spring to watch both a sunrise and a sunset. Note the time of day both take place. The first day of summer has the most daylight hours. How many hours were there between the sunrise and sunset?
3. Assign students to take a photograph (or draw a picture) of the sunset or sunrise they observe. They should include: date, time of day, and the location.

22 NATIONAL COLUMNIST'S DAY

Celebrate by:

1. Provide newspapers for students. Discuss articles written by columnists—sports, news, advice—their jobs and their by-lines.
2. Assign each student to write a column of his or her choice. Use the newspaper as a guideline.
3. Make a Happy Columnist Day card for your favorite columnist or one selected from the newspaper.

25 ERIC CARLE'S BIRTHDAY (1929-   )

Celebrate by:

1. Read Eric Carle's books, *The Hungry Caterpillar, The Grouchy Ladybug,* and *The Very Busy Spider* to the class.
2. Take students on a nature walk to see how many of these insects they can find.
3. Assign students a home project to create a puppet of one of these insects. Set aside a table or a corner of the room for an insect garden. Have students make a garden for their insect puppets with paper flowers, shredded paper grass, and net webs.
4. Have students bring other books of Eric Carle—of which he is either the illustrator or the author and illustrator.

25 VIRGINIA ADMISSION DAY

Celebrate by:

1. Virginia became the 10th state in 1788. Add this information to your United States map (page 13). Color the state lightly with colored pencil or crayon.
2. Write this state opposite its number on the State Admission Order page (page 15).

27 HELEN KELLER'S BIRTHDAY (1880–1968)

Celebrate by:

1. *See:* January, National Eye Health Care Month; May, National Hearing Month. Read a book or show a short film on the life of Helen Keller.
2. Pair students. Have them take turns drawing letters on the open palms of their partners. With eyes closed, the student must "feel" the letter. Older students can write short words.

29 YO-YO ENDURANCE RECORD BROKEN

Celebrate by:

1. On this day in 1985, Bob Brown broke the yo-yo endurance record with a time of 121 hours and 10 minutes. Ask your parent group to provide a yo-yo for each student. Allow a few days for practice.
2. Provide timers and stop watches. Pair the students. Let them monitor each other for the "finals." See how long each student can keep his or her yo-yo going. Have the monitor record the time on a class chart. Older students can figure out how much longer Bob Brown's record was than their own.
3. Write a "tall tale" about how, when, where, and why YOU invented the yo-yo.

HOLEY DONUT CARD

Color and cut out the donut. Cut out the small hole.

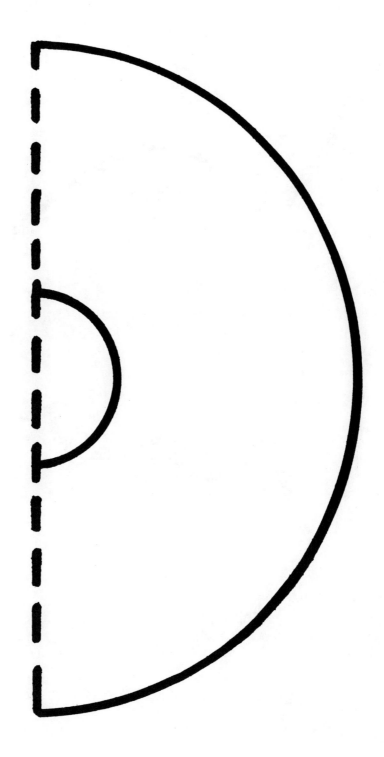

DOUBLE EAGLE

Cut out the eagle. Add thick paint and use your finger to trace feather designs into the paint.

July

Flower – Water lily
Birthstone – Ruby

July is the seventh month of the year. It was the fifth month in the Ancient Roman calendar. Julius Ceasar was born this month, and after his death, the Roman Senate changed the name of the month to July in honor of his memory. July has thirty-one days.

MONTH

ANTI-BOREDOM MONTH
Celebrate by:
1. Discuss the meaning of bored or boredom. Have each student write down one thing he or she finds boring in his or her life and why it is boring (do not put names on the papers). Collect the papers.
2. Pass out the papers at random. Have students write down advice on how to deal with the boredom problem. Collect the papers. Read the papers to the class.
3. Discuss things students can do to avoid becoming bored.

NATIONAL BAKED BEAN MONTH
Celebrate by:
1. Have students bring in examples of dried beans and identify them.
2. Combine the beans, wash, and cook them in the microwave, on the stove, or in a crock pot. Add seasoning.
3. Serve the beans in paper cups. Have students identify the beans and describe the differences in taste.
4. Purchase cans of baked beans. Heat as directed and save. Compare the baked beans to the beans you cooked in activities #2 and #3.

NATIONAL HOT DOG MONTH
Celebrate by:
1. Visit a meat market and find out how hot dogs are made and the differences among the kinds of hot dogs. Purchase a few.
2. Cut the hot dogs in small pieces and serve on toothpicks. Have students write down the varieties and a comparison of the tastes.

NATIONAL ICE CREAM MONTH

Celebrate by:

1. *See:* 3rd Sunday in July, National Ice Cream Day; September 22, Ice Cream Cone Invented. Check with parents for a hand-crank ice cream freezer and make ice cream the old fashioned way.
2. Make ice cream in a freezer tray; make sherbet in a freezer tray. Ask parents for help in donating ingredients, and get permission for use of the freezer in the cafeteria.
3. Compare the two kinds of ice cream; compare the ice cream to sherbet.

NATIONAL BLUEBERRY MONTH

Celebrate by:

1. Make a list of the different kinds of berries. Bring in pictures of berries to decorate a bulletin board.
2. Bring in fresh blueberries for a sample taste. Make blueberry muffins using a muffin mix. Compare the canned blueberries in the package mix to the fresh berries.
3. Read the rhyming book, *Jamberry*, by Bruce Degen (Harper Trophy). Have students write an additional page or two for the book.

NATIONAL RECREATION AND PARKS MONTH

Celebrate by:

1. Blow up a map of your state for each student. Locate and mark the national parks.
2. Have students make a booklet listing the national parks in your area or state. List other recreational sites (lakes, beaches, picnic areas) and their locations. Encourage students to share the booklet with their families and plan to visit one of the places.
3. Have each student write to a recreational facility or park in your state for visitor's information. Set up a display.
4. Pick up litter at a nearby park or one in your neighborhood. Tally the recyclables people leave in the park—bottles, cans, glass, etc.

NATIONAL TENNIS MONTH

Celebrate by:

1. Draw a picture of a tennis racket, ball and net.
2. Discuss the game of tennis, the rules and equipment needed to play the game.
3. Make a class list of all the equipment one would need if one decided to take up tennis. Have each student copy the list, check a catalog or sporting goods store for the price of each item, and add the total cost of the equipment.
4. If a court and equipment are available, enlist the help of tennis-playing parents to give a demonstration and help the students learn the game.

READ AN "ALMANAC" MONTH

Celebrate by:

1. What is an almanac? Bring in as many types as possible for students to look through—nautical almanacs, the *United Nations Almanac*, the *Farmer's Almanac*, the *World Almanac*.
2. Have students make a list of information one can find in an almanac. Share one fact from an almanac with the class.

1st week FREEDOM WEEK

Celebrate by:

1. *See:* February 1, National Freedom Day, proclaimed by President Harry S. Truman.
   Ask for a definition of the words freedom and liberty. Ask how the two terms differ.
2. Have each student write a short essay on "What Freedom Means to Me." Send copies to the
   local newspaper editor to see if they might be printed.
3. Have students research: President Franklin D. Roosevelt's "four freedoms," a message given
   in 1941; President Abraham Lincoln's Emancipation Proclamation on January 1, 1863; and
   the outlawing of slavery Lincoln signed on February 1, 1865.

DAY

1 BUREAU OF INTERNAL REVENUE ESTABLISHED (1862)

See: April 15, Income Tax Pay-Day. The bureau of Internal Revenue was established by an act
of Congress on this date. The purpose was to help pay for the cost of the Civil War. The IRS head-
quarters are in Washington, DC.

1 UNITED STATES STAMP ANNIVERSARY

Celebrate by:

1. The first adhesive-backed United States postage stamps were issued by the United States
   Postal Service on this day in 1847. Display in a plastic sleeve, different denominations of
   stamps and discuss them.
2. Borrow a postal scale to share with students. Have them bring in "junk mail" letters. Fold
   one, two, three, and more pieces of paper together. Estimate the amount of postage and write
   it on each group of folded paper. Cut stamps from different colors of construction paper and
   assign a denomination to each color. Weigh the folded papers, check with your estimates, and
   affix the correct postage.
3. Give each student a copy of "Stamp It!" (page 107) to complete.
   Answer: Zoning Improvement Plan

1 UNITED STATES FIRST ZOO ESTABLISHED

Celebrate by:

1. The Philadelphia Zoological Society opened the first zoo in the United States on this day in
   1874. Students will enjoy *If I Ran the Zoo* by Dr. Seuss (Random House).
2. Have each student write a paragraph on what he or she thinks is the purpose of a zoo.
3. List on a class chart, animals that are found in a zoo.
4. Zoo is a short form for zoological garden; zoology is the study of animal life. Why do you
   think we call these places zoos?
5. If students have visited zoos, have them share some experiences.
6. If one is nearby, visit a zoo, or have a docent come and speak to the class.
7. Debate whether or not wild animals should be kept in zoos.

3 FIRST BANK OPENED IN THE UNITED STATES (1791)

Celebrate by:

1. The first bank to open in the United States was called: The First National Bank for Savings. Name some of the banks in your city.
2. On a classroom chart, make a list of services provided by banks.
3. Give each student a copy of "Bank Order" (page 108) to complete.

3 IDAHO ADMISSION DAY

Celebrate by:

1. Idaho became the 43rd state in 1890. Add this information to your United States map (page 13). Color the state lightly with colored pencil or crayon.
2. Write this state opposite its number on the State Admission Order page (page 15).

4 AMERICA THE BEAUTIFUL PUBLISHED (1895)

See: July 22, America The Beautiful. This poem by Katharine Lee Bates was first published in a Congregational church publication.

4 INDEPENDENCE DAY

Celebrate by:

1. This day is our nation's birthday. It is also called Fourth of July and Firecracker Day. Sing Happy Birthday to America.
2. On this date in 1776, the Declaration of Independence was approved. The official signing was on August 2, 1776. How many years have passed since the signing? On what date was our country's 200th anniversary? How long ago was this?
3. Play patriotic music and have students suggest patriotic songs to sing.
4. Secure a copy of the Declaration of Independence from an encyclopedia or history book to share with the students. Read, and discuss, the Preamble with the class.

4 GREAT SEAL OF THE UNITED STATES ANNIVERSARY (1776)

See: June 20, Bald Eagle Becomes Official Symbol. After voting to adopt the Declaration of Independence, the Continental Congress formed a committee to plan for the seal of the United States of America. Six years later, on June 20, 1782, the bald eagle became our official symbol.

10 WYOMING ADMISSION DAY

Celebrate by:

1. Wyoming became the 44rd state in 1890. Add this information to your United States map (page 13). Color the state lightly with colored pencil or crayon.
2. Write this state opposite its number on the State Admission Order page (page 15).

3rd Sunday NATIONAL ICE CREAM DAY

Celebrate by:

1. This day, also called "Sundae Sunday," is a celebration to promote America's favorite dessert—ice cream. Make a list of different ways ice cream is served. Provide vanilla ice cream and assorted toppings for students to make their own sundaes.
2. Write a recipe on "how to make the best ice cream sundae in the world."

3rd weekend INTERNATIONAL JUGGLERS' ASSOCIATION ANNUAL FESTIVAL

Celebrate by:

1. This event, held Tuesday through Saturday of the third full week of July, has been held in Fargo, North Dakota, since 1947. Which anniversary does this year mark?
2. Provide materials for practicing juggling such as balls, bean bags, hoops, plastic Indian clubs, and yarn balls. Later you may want to provide stop watches to see how long a person can juggle. This is a good activity for developing eye-hand coordination, timing, and balance.
3. After some practice, have students work with a partner to juggle items back and forth.

20 APOLLO MOON LANDING (1969)

Celebrate by:

1. On this date Neil Armstrong and Edwin Eugene Aldrin, Jr., landed lunar module *Eagle*, at 4:17 p.m. Eastern Daylight Time. What time was this where you live? Which anniversary are we celebrating today?
2. Neil Armstrong was the first to set foot on the moon. For approximately two hours and fifteen minutes, he walked on the surface of the moon. What were the famous words he sent back to earth? ("That's one small step for a man, one giant leap for mankind.")

22 AMERICA THE BEAUTIFUL ANNIVERSARY

Celebrate by:

1. The words were written by Katharine Lee Bates—teacher, poet, and author. She wrote her famous words after riding a mule cart to the top of Pikes Peak on July 22, 1893. Find Pikes Peak on a map (near Colorado Springs, Colorado). How many years is it since she first wrote these words?
2. Katharine was born in Falmouth, Massachusetts, in 1859. See what else you can find out about this remarkable woman who spoke many languages and traveled around the world.
3. Read all the verses of the song to the class and have them sing the first verse.
4. Have each student make a list and illustrate some of the beautiful places he or she has seen in America.

26 NEW YORK ADMISSION DAY

1. New York became the 11th state in 1788. Add this information to your United States map (page 13). Color the state lightly with colored pencil or crayon.
2. Write this state opposite its number on the State Admission Order page (page 15).

26 PIED PIPER OF HAMELIN (1284 or 1376)

Celebrate by:

1. Read the fairy tale and then have students see what they can find out about the Pied Piper of Hamelin.
2. Find Hamelin, Germany, on the map.
3. Select a Pied Piper and divide the rest of the class into the children, the mice, and the towns-people and have them recreate the story.
4. Give students copies of the "Pied Piper Puppets" (page 110) to decorate, cut out and paste on one end of a wooden paint stirring stick (or strip of heavy cardboard). Read the story and have students act out the roles using puppets.

30 VLADIMIR KOSMA ZWORYKIN'S BIRTHDAY (1889– 1982)

Celebrate by:

1. Write this man's name on the chalkboard. Have students write down the answers to the fol-lowing multiple choices:
   Vladimir Zworykin was the: a) Father of Television, b) first man in space, c) first Zsar of Russia *(answer: a)*
   He was born in: a) Germany, b) Russia, c) Poland *(answer: b)*
   He was: a) a president, b) a scientist, c) a medical doctor *(answer: b)*
   Have students see if they can find the answers through research.
2. Challenge students to go for a week (or five days) without watching any television, and then share their experiences.
3. Provide copies of "A Date With TV" (page 111) for students to complete.

TYPEWRITER INVENTED 1829, (the exact day in July is unknown)

Celebrate by:

1. William Burt of Michigan had the first American patent for a typewriter. He called it a "typographer." Thomas Edison improved on Burt's invention by substituting metal parts for wooden ones. Before Edison's improvements, a person could write faster by hand than with the machine. Visit your school office and examine a typewriter. See if there is an electric, stan-dard, and automatic typewriter at the school that can be used for a comparison. Ask a secre-tary how many words per minute he or she can type. Can you write this fast? Upon return-ing to the classroom, let students see how many words they can write by hand in a minute.
2. Compare a typewriter to a word processor or computer.
3. Try to locate a portable or other standard typewriter to bring to class. Let students take turns trying it out.

July 1—UNITED STATES STAMP ANNIVERSARY STAMP IT!

Postal Cards were first issued in 1873. The already stamped card cost one cent.

Today postal cards cost _____ cents.

How much more does a postal card cost today than in 1873? _____

At one time you could send a letter for three cents.

Today a first class stamp costs _____ cents.

How much more does a first class stamp cost today? _____

The first regular air mail service in the world began in 1918. Find out if the first mail service was between New York City and Washington, DC; between New York City and Los Angeles; or between New York City and Chicago.

When you address a letter, don't forget the ZIP or Zip Code. Zip codes were started in 1963 to improve mail deliver. What do the letters ZIP stand for?

July 3—FIRST BANK OPENED IN THE UNITED STATES
BANK ORDER

The names of five banks and their founding dates (dates they first opened) are listed in the boxes. Cut the boxes apart and paste them in order of the dates they were founded.

Wells Fargo Bank **1852**	**1**
Bank of America **1904**	**2**
City Bank **1812**	**3**
First National Bank **1863**	**4**
Chase Manhattan Bank **1799**	**5**

Name _____

July 26—PIED PIPER OF HAMELIN
PIED PIPER PUPPETS

July 30—VLADIMIR KOSMA ZWORYKIN'S BIRTHDAY
A DATE WITH TV

Vladimir Zworykin was a Russian-born scientist. He demonstrated the first completely electronic television system in 1929. Find out some important events and changes that have taken place in television since 1929. Fill in the time line.

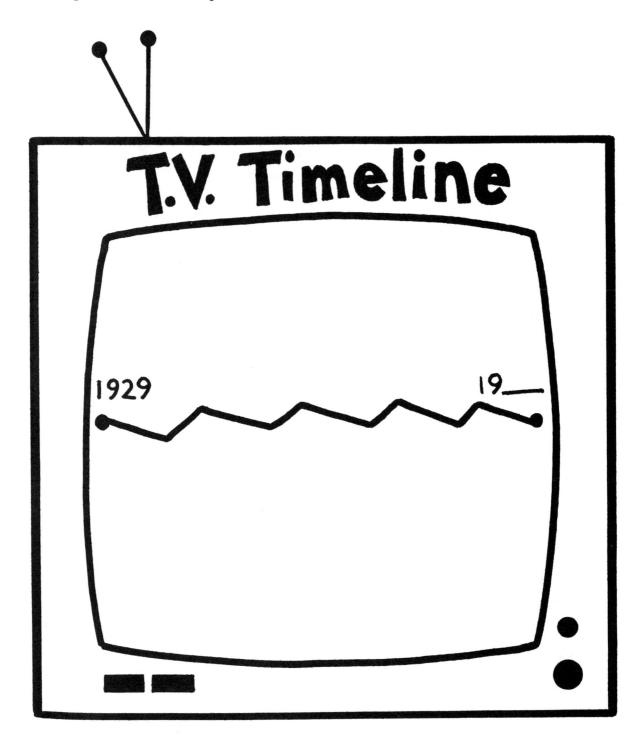

August

Flower – Poppy and gladiolus
Birthstone – Sardonyx and peridot

August is the eighth month of the year. It was the sixth month in the Roman calendar. August was originally called Sextilis which means sixth. August was named after Augustus (which means exalted), the emperor of Rome, and was the name given to Julius Caesar when he became the first Emperor of Rome. August has thirty-one days.

WEEK

1-7 NATIONAL CLOWN WEEK
Celebrate by:
1. A clown is a comedian, usually associated with a circus, who performs straight pantomime. Some clowns have their own acts. Read about some of the famous clowns such as Emmett Kelly, Red Skeleton, Felix Adler, and Lou Jacobs.
2. Plan a clown day during the week. Have students do tricks, juggle, pantomime, or perform other acts. Make costumes from paper bags, boxes, newspapers, and old clothing. Ask a parent to come in and do face painting for those who would like their faces painted.
3. Give each student a copy of "Puzzling Clown" (page 117) to complete. Instruct students as to the number of pieces into which they are to cut the puzzle.

1st week NATIONAL SMILE WEEK
Celebrate by:
1. "Share a smile and it will come back to you" is a slogan based on National Smile Week. Make a poster using this slogan.
2. Provide hand mirrors for students and let them practice smiling at themselves.
3. Read a humorous picture book to the class. Pause now and then and say, "smile."

3rd week BE KIND TO HUMANKIND WEEK
Celebrate by:
1. This is a special week to be caring and considerate of others. Write a note to a friend, teacher or family member, thanking him or her for some act of kindness toward you or someone else.
2. Have students write down the following "Kindness Ideas" from the Organization of Humankind Week.

> Sacrifice Our Wants for Others' Needs Sunday
> Motorist Consideration Monday
> Touch-A-Heart Tuesday
> Willing to Lend a Hand Wednesday
> Thoughtful Thursday
> Favors Granted Friday
> Speak Kind Words Saturday

Discuss how we can exercise these suggestions. Challenge students to put them in practice for a week (in hopes they will continue the practice).

4th week LITTLE LEAGUE BASEBALL WORLD SERIES

Celebrate by:

1. *See:* 2nd week of June, National Little League Baseball Week. The World Series is held in Williamsport, Pennsylvania. Eight teams from around the world play for the World Championship.
2. Find Williamsport on the map. If one decides to fly to see the World Series, what would be the closest major city to Williamsport? How many states would one have to fly across to get there?

DAY

1 COLORADO ADMISSION DAY

Celebrate by:

1. Colorado became the 38th state in 1876. Add this information to your United States map (page 13). Color the state lightly with colored pencil or crayon.
2. Write this state opposite its number on the State Admission Order page (page 15).

1 FRANCIS SCOTT KEY'S BIRTHDAY (1779–1843)

Celebrate by:

1. *See:* March 3, National Anthem Day. Francis Scott Key was the author of America's national anthem. What is our national anthem?
2. Give each student a copy of "Francis Scott Key's Birthday" (page 116) to complete. Play an instrumental recording of "The Star Spangled Banner," while students are working.
3. Sing "The Star Spangled Banner."
4. Draw a picture showing the flag as the author saw it on that early morning.

1st Sunday FRIENDSHIP DAY

Celebrate by:

1. Friendship Day was sanctioned by Congress in 1935. Have each student list five things he or she looks for in a friend.
2. Have students write a poem about their best friends.
3. Have students take turns introducing a classmate without giving the name. Have students guess who it is.
4. Today, introduce yourself to a new friend, an adult, or student at school whom you do not know.

2 KID'S SWAP SHOP DAY

Celebrate by:

1. This event is held annually in Baltimore, Maryland. Have each student bring one item, concealed in a paper bag, to swap. Set your own guidelines such as something you would want to receive in a swap, and nothing living. Swaps should be made without looking into the bag. After swapping, students can keep the items or continue swapping for a specified time.
2. Have each student who wishes to swap, bring in one used book in good condition. Set aside a time for book swapping.

4 COAST GUARD DAY
Celebrate by:
1. Anniversary of the founding of the United States Coast Guard, a branch of the armed services (1790). Discuss the Coast Guard—where it is located, its duties, and how its members help people.
2. Find out if students or their families have ever received help from the Coast Guard, or if they know any one who is or has been a member of this branch of the armed services.
3. Draw a picture of a Coast Guard ship, called a cutter, involved in a sea rescue operation.

8 AMERICAN FAMILY DAY
Celebrate by:
1. Discuss family reunions. Have each student make a list of all the relatives he or she would invite for a family reunion for one side of the family.
2. Have each student write about how his or her family spends weekends or vacations.
3. Give each student a copy of "My Family Tree" (page 118) to complete.

9 SMOKEY THE BEAR'S BIRTHDAY
Celebrates by:
1. Make copies of "Smokey's Birthday Quiz" (page 119) for each student.
2. Smokey first appeared on his famous poster on this date in 1944. Make posters to celebrate Smokey's birthday. Students can add their own slogans. Display the posters in the cafeteria, library, or stores and business places around town.

10 MISSOURI ADMISSION DAY
Celebrate by:
1. Missouri became the 24th state in 1821. Add this information to your United States map (page 13). Color the state lightly with colored pencil or crayon.
2. Write this state opposite its number on the State Admission Order page (page 15).

13 INTERNATIONAL LEFT-HANDER'S DAY
Celebrate by:
1. Survey the class to see how many students or family members are left-handed. Explain how left-handedness often runs in families and is more prevalent in boys. Ask if this is true in your survey. Discuss some of the advantages and disadvantages of being left-handed.
2. Research and do a report on a left-handed sports figure, musician, physician, scientist, or other person who has made a major contribution to society.

14 MIDDLE CHILDREN'S DAY
Celebrate by:
1. Have students write down what they feel would be two advantages and two disadvantages of being the middle child in a family (this could include children in a three child family or more). Let all the "middle child in a family" children form a panel. As students read their lists, have the panel make comments.
2. Divide the students into pairs or small groups. Have each group visit an assigned class and take a survey of the "middle" children in each class. Use the survey information to compile a graph.

14 V-J DAY
Celebrate by:

1. *See:* December 7, Pearl Harbor Day. Point out some of the countries involved. V-J Day stands for Victory over Japan, the end of WWII. This date is based on an informal agreement and is celebrated in the United States on August 14. The date the Japanese surrendered to the Allies was September 2, 1945. The surrender was signed aboard the USS Missouri in Tokyo Bay. Find Japan on a map, locate Tokyo Bay.
2. Discuss (or explain) who the Allies were and how the war in the Pacific started.

15 NATIONAL RELAXATION DAY
Celebrate by:

1. Discuss what it means to relax. Have students show you a relaxed state in both a sitting and a standing position.
2. Ask for words that describe the opposite of relaxed. Have students sit and tense all their muscles, starting from toes to head as you call out the body parts—"tighten your toes and feet, your legs," and so on—and then "relax completely."
3. Compare how you feel when your muscles are tight and tense to when they are relaxed.

19 NATIONAL AVIATION DAY and ORVILLE WRIGHT'S BIRTHDAY (1871–1948)
Celebrate by:

1. *See:* December 17, Wright Brothers' First Powered Flight. Using your own design, make a paper glider or airplane (provide books or give directions for folding for younger children).
2. Bring in pictures of airplanes for the bulletin board. Try to identify each plane with a name tag beside it.

20 HAWAII ADMISSION DAY
Celebrate by:

1. Hawaii became the 50th state in 1959. Add this information to your United States map (page 13). Color the state lightly with colored pencil or crayon.
2. Write this state opposite its number on the State Admission Order page (page 15).

27 FIRST OIL WELL DRILLED (1859)
Celebrate by:

1. W.A. "Uncle Billy" Smith is given credit for drilling the first oil well in the United States. Do you think it was in Texas, California, or Pennsylvania? (It was in Titusville, Pennsylvania.) Check to see if there are any oil wells or refineries in your area or your state.
2. Discuss products made from oil or petroleum. Check dictionaries and encyclopedias. Bring in pictures of these products for the bulletin board.
3. Give each student a copy of "Black Gold" (page 120) to complete.
4. Have students try to locate books on oil, oil drilling, or petroleum products such as *Oil; The Buried Treasure* by Roma Gans (Harper); *Oil* by Barbara Lowery (Watts); *Oil* by Harland Wade (Raintree).

30 Anniversary of the FIRST BABY BORN IN THE WHITE HOUSE (1893)

Celebrate by:

1. Older students might like to guess which president's wife had the first baby born in the White House. Frances Folsom Cleveland (Mrs. Grover Cleveland) was the first president's wife to have a baby in the White House—a baby girl named Ester. Ester was not the first child born in the White House. That was one of Thomas Jefferson's granddaughters born in 1806. How many years was that before Ester was born?
2. Make a list of the names of recent children who live or have lived in the White House while their father was president.
3. Have students write essays on what it would be like to live in the White House if one of their parents were the President.

Name _____

August 1—FRANCIS SCOTT KEY'S BIRTHDAY

Francis Scott Key wrote our national anthem. What is the name of our national anthem? _____

Was it first written as a letter, a poem or a song? _____

It did not become our national anthem until 117 years after it was written. On March 3, 19 _____, President _____ _____ signed an act that made it our national anthem.

Francis Scott Key was born August 1, 17 _____ in the state of _____. He died on January 11, 18 _____.

How did Francis Scott Key come to write the words that later became our national anthem?

_____

_____

_____

_____

August 1–7—NATIONAL CLOWN WEEK

PUZZLING CLOWN

Color the clown puzzle. Cut out around the frame. Glue the framed clown onto tagboard. Cut the puzzle into pieces as directed by the teacher.

Name _____

August 8—AMERICAN FAMILY DAY — MY FAMILY TREE

August 9—SMOKEY THE BEAR'S BIRTHDAY

SMOKEY'S BIRTHDAY QUIZ

Smokey was born in 1944. What is his famous slogan?

Smokey's friend appeared in 1971. What is his name?

Who is the oldest?

By how many years?

How old are you?

How many years older than you is Smokey?

How many years older than you is his friend?

Name _____

August 27—FIRST OIL WELL DRILLED

BLACK GOLD

The figures inside each state represent the number of barrels of oil that states produced in one year. Check your map to find the name of the state. Write the name of the state under the number inside that state. List the names of the states to show the number of barrels of oil produced, from highest to lowest.

1st _____

2nd _____

3rd _____

4th _____

5th _____

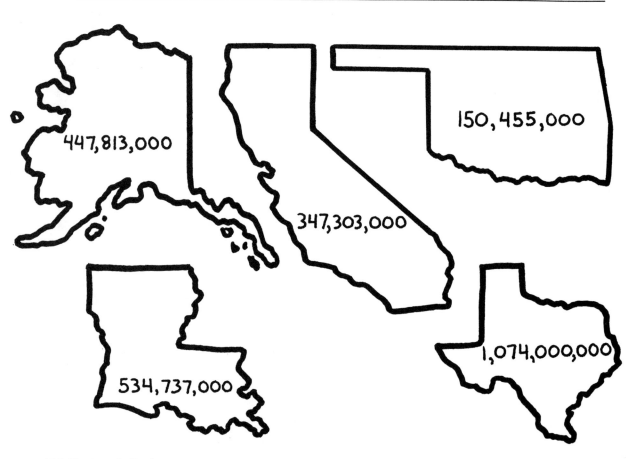

September

Flower – Morning glory
Birthstone – Sapphire

September is the ninth month of the year. In the Old Roman Calendar, it was the seventh month. The Latin word "septem" means seven. September has always had 30 days.

MONTH

EMERGENCY MEDICAL CARE MONTH
Celebrate by:
1. *Quiz:* What is the emergency telephone number? When should you dial 911? What information should you be ready to give the operator when you dial 911?
2. Explain and then demonstrate, or have someone demonstrate, the Heimlich maneuver.
3. Contact an ambulance or paramedic service to see if they will bring their unit to school.
4. Have students draw pictures of their houses, the nearest fire hydrants, medical clinics or hospitals, and fire stations.

LIBRARY CARD SIGN-UP MONTH
Celebrate by:
1. This special month is a national effort to sign up every child for a library card. It is sponsored by the National Library Association. Ask students why they think this group wants every child to have a library card. Find out how many students have library cards. Explain how to apply for a card and encourage students to do so.
2. Visit your local library. Have students who wish, apply for library cards. Ask the children's librarian to explain a card owner's responsibility. Check out books to read.

NATIONAL CHICKEN MONTH
Celebrate by:
1. *See:* September 9, Colonel Sander's Birthday; 2nd week of April, Egg Salad Week. Discuss the differences between a chicken and a turkey (and other edible fowl such as duck, goose, and pheasant). Discuss the difference between the tastes in the meats of these two birds.
2. Make a list of ways to serve chicken.
3. Bring in a dressed chicken that still has the head and feet attached, and use for a science lesson. Cut up the chicken, explaining parts as you do so. Invite a parent to come and help the class make chicken soup (with rice). While the students are eating, read *Chick Soup and Rice* by Maurice Sendak (Harper).

NATIONAL CHOLESTEROL EDUCATION MONTH
Celebrate by:
1. Discuss cholesterol—what it is, where it is found, why our bodies need it, and how and where it is manufactured in our bodies.
2. Ask a doctor or nurse for a sample read-out that shows the cholesterol level of the blood.
3. From a newspaper ad section or magazine, cut out five favorite food pictures. Glue them to a sheet of paper. Find out the amount of cholesterol in a serving of each. Write the amount under the food picture.

NATIONAL COURTESY MONTH
Celebrate by:
1. Ask students the meaning of the word courtesy. Then make a list of some ways students can express courtesy. Make a list of courtesy rules for your class.
2. Make copies of the "Courtesy Certificate." (page 130) At the end of each week, throughout the month, give certificates to students whom you have observed as being courteous.
3. At the end of the month, take a vote to see if courtesy has improved during National Courtesy Month. Encourage children to continue this behavior at school, home, and in the community.

NATIONAL HONEY MONTH
Celebrate by:
1. Invite a beekeeper, called an apiarist, to visit and demonstrate his or her beekeeping equipment.
2. Display a jar of strained honey and a jar of honey containing a piece of honeycomb. Serve honey on crackers and compare the two tastes. Read the labels to find out what the flavors are. Does the flavor tell one from where the honey came?
3. Give each student a copy of "Busy Honeybee" (page 131) to complete.

NATIONAL PIANO MONTH
Celebrate by:
1. Arrange for a piano tuner to visit and explain the mechanics of a piano.
2. Enlist the help of a pianist, teacher, parent, or friend, to come and play a variety of piano music. If any students can play, ask if they would play a piece.
3. Explain the keyboard. Discuss other instruments that have keyboards. Compare the instruments—sound, size, number of keys.

NATIONAL RICE MONTH
Celebrate by:
1. Rice is the world's most important food crop. Ask students to comment on this statement. Make a list of rice products.
2. Measure and cook two cups (or more) of rice. Have students estimate the number of cups of cooked rice there will be after the two cups are cooked. Measure the cooked rice and compare the amount to the estimates.
3. Use the cooked rice to make rice pudding. Set out the following ingredients and utensils: paper cups, plastic spoons, measuring cups and spoons, and the recipe written on folded, stand-up 3" x 5" cards—rice 1/4 cup; milk 1/4 cup; sugar 1/2 teaspoon; cinnamon 1/4 teaspoon; raisins 10. Measure the ingredients into the cup, stir, and eat!

WEEK

1st week NATIONAL DO-IT-YOURSELF WEEK
Celebrate by:
1. Have students think about things at home that they can do or fix themselves. Have them make a list of things they will try to do, such as fix or repair their toys or bikes, or help younger children fix something that needs repair.
2. Students can make their own beds, lunches, or snacks. They can ask permission to make cookies, a salad, or sandwich. At the end of the week, share things students have done by themselves for the first time.

17–23 CONSTITUTION WEEK
Celebrate by:
1. *See:* September 17, Constitution of the United States Anniversary. A Presidential Proclamation has been issued for the week of September 17–23 each year since 1955.
2. Have students look up one of the Amendments to the Constitution and copy it onto a piece of paper to read to the class.
3. Challenge older students to memorize the Preamble to the Constitution.

3rd week NATIONAL DOG WEEK
Celebrate by:
1. On a classroom chart, list the names of different breeds of dogs. Take a vote on the students' favorite.
2. Arrange to have a police, seeing-eye, or show dog brought to school for a demonstration. Make a list of ten questions the class would like to ask the dog owner or handler.

Week of the 25th RELIGIOUS FREEDOM WEEK
Celebrate by:
1. The week of September 25 is proclaimed by Congressional Resolution and Presidential Proclamation as Religious Freedom Week. Ask students what religious freedom means and write the comments on a classroom chart.
2. Read and discuss the first Amendment to the Constitution.
3. Write a paragraph on how individuals in our nation would be affected if we did not have religious freedom in the United States.

4 PETER RABBIT'S BIRTHDAY (1893)
Celebrate by:
1. Beatrix Potter (1866–1943) of England wrote a letter in 1893 to a friend's invalid son. She wrote the letter/story about a rabbit named Peter and Mr. McGregor who had a garden. The letter later became her first book. What was the title of this book? Find England on the map.
2. Write a story/letter to a friend.
3. What year did Peter Rabbit celebrate his 100th birthday? How long ago was it? How old was Beatrix Potter when she wrote *Peter Rabbit*? How old was she when she died?
4. Give each student a copy of "The Great Garden Maze" (page 132) to complete.

4 NEWSPAPER CARRIER DAY
Celebrate by:
1. *See:* June 22, National Columnist Day; 2nd week in October, National Newspaper Week. Ten year old Barney Flatherty became the first "newsboy" in 1833. Find out the name of your local newspaper carrier and write him or her a "Happy Newspaper Carrier Day" card.
2. Find out how many students (or family members) are or have been newspaper carriers. What time does a newspaper carrier have to get up in the morning? How many papers do they carry? How old does one have to be? If no one in class can answer the questions, assign students to interview a carrier and find out.

1st Monday LABOR DAY
Celebrate by:
1. What is Labor Day and why is it a holiday? On June 28, 1894, a president signed a bill making Labor Day an official holiday. Who was that president? (Grover Cleveland) Congress designated the first Monday in September as our National Labor Day Holiday. The purpose was to honor the working people.
2. How do you and your family celebrate Labor Day?

8 INTERNATIONAL LITERACY DAY
Celebrate by:
1. International Literacy Day is a special day to make us aware of the need to be literate. What does this mean? To be literate means we can think, read, write, and spell words. Read, read, and read today and everyday.
2. Students can keep a list of the titles of all books, magazines, and newspapers they read for a week. They can rate themselves. Did they read—none, a little, lots, or a great deal?
3. Have students read a newspaper comic strip to a younger child.
4. Students can read a story or a short article from a magazine to an adult.

9 COLONEL SANDER'S BIRTHDAY (1890–1980)

Celebrate by:

1. *See:* September, National Chicken Month. Was Colonel Sanders a real person? (Yes, Colonel Harland David Sanders was the founder of the Kentucky Fried Chicken Chain.)
2. Visit one of the stores and find out where they get their chickens; how a person can have their own store (franchise); and what is on the menu.
3. Have students write poems about their visit.

10 SWAP IDEAS DAY

Celebrate by:

1. Discuss the word "idea." Why do we need new ideas?
2. Work in small groups to see what new ideas students can come up with for their school. Talk about the ideas and decide on two that are realistic, worthwhile and helpful. Present the "new ideas" to the principal.

11 FIRST CARTOON STRIP (1875)

Celebrate by:

1. Bring in your favorite cartoon strip, read it to the class, tell why it is your favorite, and then attach it to the bulletin board.
2. The name of the first comic strip was, "Professor Tigwissel's Burglar Alarm." What do you think might have been the storyline?
3. Bring in a comic strip, with the text removed, for each student. Have them paste the comic strips across the bottoms of sheets of paper and then write the text to go with the pictures.
4. Have older students write, illustrate their own comic strips and name them.

11 CHAMPION EGG LAYER

Celebrate by:

1. *See:* May, National Egg Month; 2nd week of April, Egg Salad Week. On this day in 1971, Penny, a Rhode Island Red hen, laid seven eggs. Ask if anyone can explain what is unusual about Penny's feat. (Chickens usually lay one, sometimes two eggs on any one day.)
2. A Rhode Island Red is a breed of chicken. Do you know the names of any other breeds? Check the encyclopedia or other sources.

1st Sunday following Labor Day NATIONAL GRANDPARENT'S DAY

Celebrate by:

1. *See:* August 8, American Family Day. Grandparent's Day was first proclaimed on September 6, 1979. Take a survey of the students to see how many living grandparents are represented. Provide 2-inch squares of tagboard for writing the names of each grandparent, great-grandparent, and so on.
2. Hang clothesline from one corner of the room to the other. Have each student write his or her name on a square of paper, and staple it to the top of a piece of yarn. Staple the grandparent cards in a line beneath his or her name. Tie the yarn to the clothesline.

15 WORLD'S LARGEST WEATHER VANE ANNIVERSARY

Celebrate by:

1. Ask, "What is a weather vane (also called a wind vane) and where would we find one?"
2. The world's largest weather vane was built September 15, 1984. It was 48-feet high, with a 26-foot wind arrow, weighed 3,500 pounds, and was built in Montague, Michigan.
3. Look at pictures of weather vanes. On the blacktop or sidewalk, use a long measuring tape to measure 48-feet for the height, and an arrow 26-feet in length. Help the students trace in a weather vane with wide chalk.
4. Bring to class a bathroom scale and weigh each student. Record the weight of each on the chalkboard. How much more, or less, was the total weight of the students than the world's largest weather vane?

16 NATIONAL PLAY-DOH DAY (1955)

Celebrate by:

1. Play-Doh was first introduced on this day in 1955. Provide different colors of Play-Doh for students to create something of their choice.
2. Bring in craft books for students to look through to find play dough recipes. Have students work in small groups and write down as many recipes as they can find. They may also wish to check with parents or other sources for recipes. Make a class recipe book of play doughs.
3. Assign each group a recipe. Have them plan and then bring in the ingredients needed to make the dough recipe.
4. Compare the doughs made by the groups such as in the texture and pliability. Compare them also to the commercial Play-Doh.

16 MAYFLOWER DAY

Celebrate by:

1. On this day in 1620, the Pilgrims sailed from Plymouth, England on the *Mayflower*. They landed in Plymouth, Massachusetts, on December 26, 1620. (Write the dates on the chalkboard.) How many days did it take them to get there?
2. There were 102 passengers aboard the *Mayflower*. How many students are in your class? How many more passengers were on the *Mayflower* than students in your class?
3. Have students draw a picture of how they think the *Mayflower* ship may have appeared.

17 CITIZENSHIP DAY

Celebrate by:

1. Citizenship Day is always on the same day as the anniversary of the Constitution and is celebrated during Constitution Week. What is a citizen? What is citizenship? Have students check the dictionary and read the definitions to the class.
2. Explain to the students how one becomes a citizen—by being born in this country or becoming a naturalized citizen—and what dual citizenship means.
3. List five things that make a good citizen. Have students write down two things that they will try to do to be a good citizen during this week.

17 UNITED STATES CONSTITUTION ANNIVERSARY

Celebrate by:

1. *See:* September 17–23, Constitution Week. On September 17, 1887, delegates from twelve states voted in Philadelphia to approve the proposed Constitution of the United States. Work in small groups to find out: how did the Constitution came into being; what are the names of some of the "Founding Fathers" and signers; who wrote the Constitution and where can the original be found?

18 OUR CAPITOL'S BIRTHDAY

Celebrate by:

1. George Washington laid the cornerstone for the Capitol on this date in 1793. The length of the Capitol is two football fields long. Find out how long a football field is, and then how long the Capitol is.
2. The Capitol has 540 rooms, 658 windows, 850 doorways, and 180 fireplaces. Write this information on the chalkboard and have the students copy it, listing each separately down the left side of the page. Opposite each, have them write the number of rooms, windows, doorways, and fireplaces in their houses or apartments.
3. Have each student draw a diagram of the floor plan of his or her house or apartment to show the rooms, windows, doorways, and fireplaces.
4. For older students—give each student a copy of "Inside the Capitol" (page 133) to complete.

22 BIRTHDAY OF THE ICE CREAM CONE

Celebrate by:

1. *See:* July, National Ice Cream Month; July 18, National Ice Cream Day. The first ice cream cone was made from a round, waffle cookie. Cut circles from butcher paper about 6 inches in diameter. Have students roll the circles into cone shapes, and tape the edges. Make popcorn to fill the cones.
2. Make copies of the "Ice Cream Cone" (page 134) pattern for each student. Have each cut out the cone and the ice cream, and glue ice cream to the cone.
3. Students make ice cream in their favorite flavor/color. Make cones in different colors to represent flavors and pin them across the bottom of the bulletin board. Have students pin their cut-out ice cream on top of the matching double, triple, and so on deckers.

22 or 23 AUTUMN BEGINS

Celebrate by:

1. This date is the start of the autumnal equinox. Find out what that means. Check a newspaper or almanac for the exact day and time fall begins.
2. On this date, in the Northern Hemisphere fall begins. Find the Northern Hemisphere on a world globe. What season will be starting in the Southern Hemisphere? Locate the Southern Hemisphere.
3. On this day, the sun rises due east and sets due west, causing a day with equal amounts of light and darkness. Provide compasses, explain how they always point north, and have students check the direction of the sun.

24 JIM HENSON'S BIRTHDAY (1936–1990)

Celebrate by:

1. Name Jim Henson's famous puppets (write the names on a class chart—Kermit the Frog, Big Bird, Rowlf, Bert, Ernie, Miss Piggy). Discuss what students like best about each character.
2. Provide material for making puppets. Have students work in small groups to do a puppet presentation.

24 WORLD'S LARGEST HAMBURGER

Celebrate by:

1. The world's largest hamburger was exhibited on this date in 1975. Do you think it was made in Japan, Australia, or America? (It was made in Australia and weighed 2,859 pounds.)
2. The hamburger was 27 feet around (in circumference). To show the size, have students measure 27 feet of string or yarn. Tie the two ends of the string together and have each student take hold of the yarn with both hands. Form the string into a circle and place it on the floor (or outside).
3. How can we find out how many quarter-pounders could be made from this 2,859 pound hamburger? (Multiply by 4, or add 2,859 four times.)

25 PANCAKE DAY

Celebrate by:

1. *See:* 4th week in January, National Pancake Week. Make pancakes from pancake mix. Tint the batter and pour into a squeeze bottle and squeeze out pancake shapes—heart, Christmas tree, shamrock.
2. *See:* September 22, Birthday of the Ice Cream Cone. Add mashed bananas or strawberries to the pancake batter. Try rolling a round pancake into a cone shape like the first ice cream cone
3. Give each student one small and two large, round pancakes, a paper plate, plastic knife, and ten raisins to create a pancake person.

26 JOHNNY APPLESEED'S BIRTHDAY (1774–1847)

Celebrate by:

1. What was Johnny Appleseed's real name? (John Chapman) Read or tell the story to the class.
2. *Riddle:* What would be worse than finding a worm in your apple? *Answer:* Finding half a worm! Cut two apples in half, one in each direction. Show the inside of the apples. Ask students to compare the two. Cut a pear crosswise. Both fruits cut crosswise will show the seed bed to be in the form of a star.
3. Bring in apples in different colors. Compare the apples. Cut samples for a test comparison. Use adjectives to describe the different tastes.
4. Set out a red, yellow and a green apple. Have students write down the colors and estimate the weight of each. Weigh the apples on a balance scale, and check the weight against the estimates.

4th Sunday NATIONAL GOOD NEIGHBOR DAY

Celebrate by:

1. Have each student write down the names of two to four neighbors. Write out a plan for ways you, or your family, can be a good neighbor to your neighbors. Discuss the plan with your family. Implement your plans and try hard to continue being a good neighbor.

2. If your city has a Sister City (check with the Chamber of Commerce for the name, address, the name of a school, and other information on the city)—they are usually located in another country—make plans to contact a school. Locate the country and city, if possible, on the map. Have students contribute to a class letter. Send the letter, and a photograph of the class and school, a nearby park or attraction, a class project— or whatever the class decides—to a school or class in your sister city.

COURTESY CERTIFICATE

____

name

We, your teacher and classmates appreciate your acts of courtesy shown to each of us.

We wish to congratulate you for being a courteous person.

Signed ______________________________

Date ______________________________

Name _____

September—NATIONAL HONEY MONTH

BUSY HONEYBEE

Draw a line from the word to the matching body part. Color the honeybee.

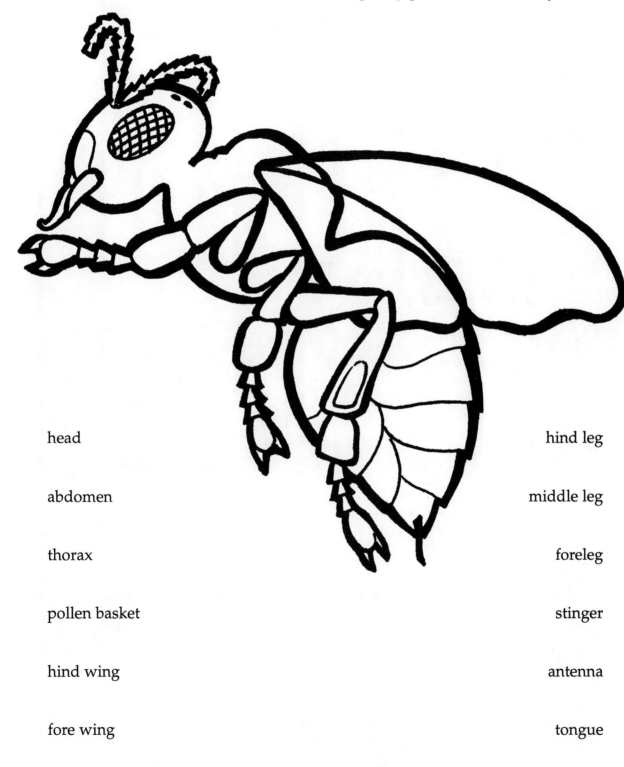

head   hind leg

abdomen   middle leg

thorax   foreleg

pollen basket   stinger

hind wing   antenna

fore wing   tongue

Name _____

September 4—PETER RABBIT'S BIRTHDAY

THE GREAT GARDEN MAZE

Can you get Peter Rabbit out of Mr. McGregor's garden?

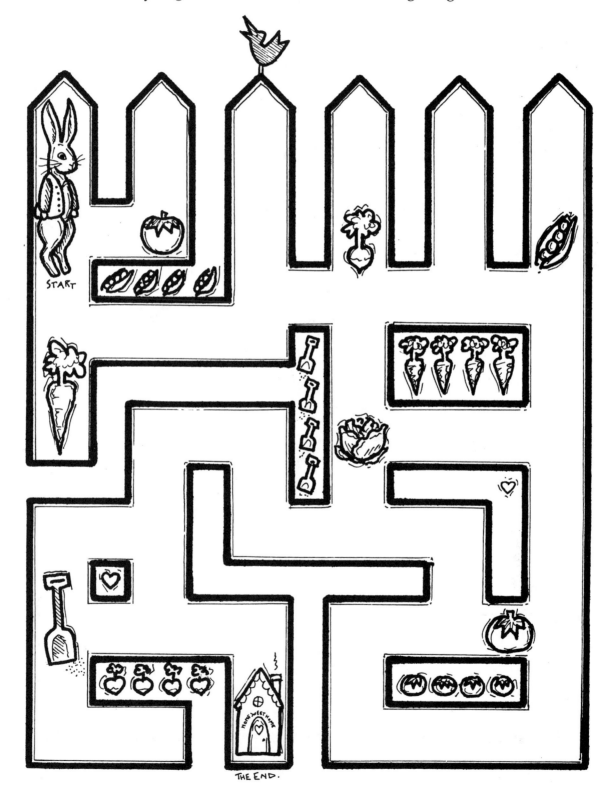

September 18—OUR CAPITOL'S BIRTHDAY

INSIDE THE CAPITOL

The Senate and the House of Representatives hold sessions in the Capitol.
Find out:

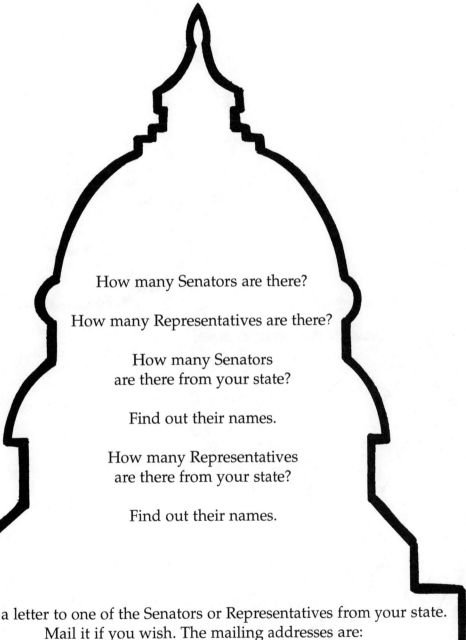

How many Senators are there?

How many Representatives are there?

How many Senators
are there from your state?

Find out their names.

How many Representatives
are there from your state?

Find out their names.

Write a letter to one of the Senators or Representatives from your state.
Mail it if you wish. The mailing addresses are:

Your Representative's Name
The U.S. House of Representatives
Washington, DC 20515

Your Senator's Name
The U.S. Senate
Washington, DC 20510

ICE CREAM CONE

October

Flower – Calendula
Birthstone – Opal and tourmaline

October is the tenth month of the year. It was the eighth month in the Roman calendar. It is called the harvest month. October has 31 days.

MONTH

ADOPT-A-SHELTER-DOG MONTH
Celebrate by:
1. The purpose of this month's celebration is to promote the adoption of puppies and dogs from local shelters. Over 50 million dogs live in the United States, however, many of them have no homes. Invite someone from your local animal shelter such as a volunteer, to speak to your class and explain how dogs can be adopted, or have students prepare questions and appoint someone to call the shelter and report back to the class.
2. Have students bring in photographs of their dogs, or cut pictures from magazines, to put on the bulletin board. Add name tags underneath each to identify the breed (or close to it). Collect as many as possible. At the end of the month, give this quiz: Which breed is the smallest (chihuahua); heaviest (St. Bernard); tallest (Irish Wolfhound)?
3. Make a list of breeds of dogs that are trained to help people. Discuss how these dogs help us and our community.

NATIONAL CLOCK MONTH
Celebrate by:
1. *See:* January 31, Official Time Began to be Kept by an Atomic Clock. Visit a clock shop and have students keep notes on the different kinds of clocks they discover.
2. Make a class list of where we might find other kinds of clocks such as in a radio, oven, microwave, and automobile.
3. Have each student estimate the number of clocks in your school. Assign small groups different areas of the school to check. Record the number of clocks and the location of each. Total all groups' totals. Compare the numbers with the students'.

NATIONAL DESSERT MONTH
Celebrate by:
1. Have each student bring in his or her favorite "kids-can-make" dessert, explain the dessert, and show how easy it is to make.
2. Decide on one or more of the recipes to make in class. Have students plan the ingredients, the amount, and the utensils needed. Then ask parents to supply what is needed.
3. Provide assorted colors of 5" x 7" cards, hole punches, and plastic rings. Have students copy five recipes they like onto cards, punch holes in one corner of the cards, and insert a ring.
4. Write the word "dessert" on the chalkboard and have students copy it onto a piece of paper. Tell them to find which letter can be removed so a new word is formed that has a different meaning (desert). Write down the new word and it's definition.

NATIONAL PIZZA MONTH

Celebrate by:

1. *See:* October 8, World's Largest Pizza. Have each student name his or her favorite topping. Then research the origin, history, and production of the favorite toppings named.
2. Find out how many different pizza franchises there are in your city (check the telephone Yellow Pages or city directory). List them on a chart.
3. Take a vote on which company makes the best pizza. Divide into groups according to choices. Allow time to discuss their company's product and to choose a spokesperson. Have each spokesperson present his or her argument.
4. Purchase a pizza from the two top companies, according to the vote, and cut them into small bite-size pieces. Number them only as #1 and #2. Have a taste test and vote again to determine the top pizza company.

NATIONAL POPCORN POPPIN' MONTH

Celebrate by:

1. Popcorn was known to the Indians of both North and South America, thousands of years ago. A North American Indian named Quadequina took a deerskin bag filled with popped corn to the first Thanksgiving celebration. Does the average popcorn kernel pop to 10, 20, or 30 times its original size? (30). Will dried fresh corn on the cob pop? Find out what is so special about popcorn that causes it to pop when other corn will not pop.
2. For a good history on popcorn and the reason it pops, read *Popcorn* by Tommy DePaola (Holiday House).
3. Set out one-fourth cup of popcorn and three bowls of distinctly different sizes. Have students estimate, by writing on a slip of paper, which bowl the popcorn will fill when popped. Test before presenting so you will have a bowl of the right capacity. Compare the results to the predictions.

NATIONAL SEAFOOD MONTH

Celebrate by:

1. On a class chart, list sea animals that are edible.
2. Have students work in pairs and choose one animal from the chart to research and then give a report.
3. Draw a picture of your favorite edible animal of the sea.
4. Provide crackers, canned tuna, and a jar of sandwich spread for students to make tuna sandwiches. Drain and mash the tuna. Add enough sandwich spread so mixture can be spread.

WEEK

1st week FIRE PREVENTION WEEK

Celebrate by:

1. This week is also *Firefighter's Week*. A Presidential Proclamation has been issued annually proclaiming the first or second week of October as Fire Prevention Week since 1925. If your school does not have a fire drill this week, plan one for the class. First review the fire drill procedures.
2. On a classroom chart, list causes of fires and ways to prevent them.
3. Discuss ways we can help firefighters. Have students write letters of appreciation to the firefighters at the stations closest to them or to the school. Mail these letters.

1st week LONDON BRIDGE DAYS

Celebrate by:

1. Have students repeat the nursery rhyme, "London Bridge is Falling Down." Explain that there was a real London Bridge, in London, England, but it was sold to a city in the United States. Ask if anyone knows where it is located or has been there and seen it. In 1967, London Bridge was torn down and sold to Lake Havasu City, Arizona, where the bridge was reconstructed.

2. Have each student contribute one question about the bridge to put in a letter. Send the letter to: Lake Havasu City Visitors' Bureau, 1930 Mesquite Avenue, Suite #3, Lake Havasu City, Arizona 86403.

1st week NATIONAL PICKLED PEPPERS' WEEK

Celebrate by:

1. On the chalkboard write, Peter Piper picked a peck of pickled peppers. Have students say the tongue-twister rapidly in unison five times.

2. Have students each write a similar tongue-twister such as Patty Patterson packed a pound of pretty pears. Have students take turns reading their tongue-twisters and having the class repeat them three to five times.

3. Discuss from where pickled peppers come. Trace peppers from the field to the pickle jar. Name other ways we use peppers.

2nd week INTERNATIONAL LETTER WRITING WEEK

Celebrate by:

1. Discuss what we could say in a letter to a child in another country if we did not know him or her.

2. Have students each select a name and write to a pen pal in another country. Find out the amount of postage needed, and contact parents or your parent group and ask if they can provide postage stamps for the letters. Students should not be required to mail their letters if they do not wish to do so.

   For a list of pen pal names and addresses, write to: U.S. Committee for UNICEF, Information Center on Children's Cultures, 331 East 38th Street, New York, New York 10016.

2nd week NATIONAL METRIC WEEK

Celebrate by:

1. *See:* December 23, Metric Conversion Act. National Metric Week was established to maintain an awareness of the metric system. Have each student bring in a clean, empty container with liquid metric markings. Provide customary measuring utensils. Have students give both the metric and customary measurements of their containers, and then prove their comparisons by using water for a demonstration.

2. Provide metric and customary measuring sticks for students to use. Explain if necessary. Assign groups of two or three students to work together, measuring objects you assign within the classroom, such as a table, bookshelf, throw rug, window, or door. Have them draw pictures of the objects and then write in both measurements.

2nd week NATIONAL SCHOOL LUNCH WEEK

Celebrate by:

1. Discuss ways to enjoy School Lunch Week.
2. Have students plan a realistic, healthy lunch menu for the week, make a shopping list and ask their parents if they can shop with them for the food.
3. Students can prepare their own lunch for the week using their own menu.

3rd week NATIONAL DENTAL HYGIENE WEEK

Celebrate by:

1. National Dental Hygiene Week was established to increase public awareness of preventive dental health care. Discuss why preventive dental care and good dental hygiene are important to our health. List the duties of a dental hygienist.
2. Provide each student with a copy of "My Tooth" (page 145) to complete. After completion, discuss the parts of a tooth.
3. The following terms are all related to the field of dentistry: oral surgery; orthodontics; prosthodontics; periodontics; and pedodontics. Assign small groups one of the terms on which to report.

3rd week NATIONAL FOREST PRODUCTS' WEEK

Celebrate by:

1. The first Presidential Proclamation for this day was in 1960 on this date. Make a class chart of products made from trees. Bring in pictures of the products on the chart and paste the picture opposite the product.
2. Make a list of things in the classroom made from trees. Discuss what it would be like if there were no trees.

3rd week NATIONAL MAGIC WEEK

Celebrate by:

1. *See:* October 31, National Magic Day. Find a picture or a story book that relates to magic in some way. Bring it to class to share.
2. Make a class list of "magic words" used in stories or in every day conversation.
3. Write a story or poem about "magic."
4. Assign students to find out who Harry Houdini was.
5. Think of some of the ways the idea of "magic" is used in advertising today, such as new, secret ingredient; magic cleaning power; washes clothes white as snow; leaves your skin smooth as silk.

DAY

2 CHARLIE BROWN AND SNOOPY'S BIRTHDAY

Celebrate by:

1. Charles Monroe Schultz's "Peanuts" comic first appeared in 1950. It now appears in 2,300 newspapers, and can be read in 26 languages throughout 68 countries. How old are Charlie Brown and Snoopy?
2. On a classroom chart, list the other characters in the comic strip. Have students work in small groups to plan how they will do imitations of one or more of the characters, and then present to the class.
3. Set up "Lucy Advice" booths. Rotate groups around the booths, changing "Lucy" so everyone gets a chance to ask and to give advice.
4. Have students write their own Snoopy's Red Baron stories. Add illustrations.

4 SPUTNIK ANNIVERSARY (1957)

Celebrate by:

1. Sputnik was the first successful man-made earth satellite. Have students find out: which country launched Sputnik; what the name means; what was the date it was launched; how much it weighed; and when did it fall to earth?
2. Find out if any students have visited any launch sites or observed any launches, or have first-hand knowledge about our space program. Ask them to share the experiences.

4 TEN-FOUR DAY

Celebrate by:

1. The fourth day of the tenth month (10-4) is a day of recognition for radio operators, to whom the code words "ten-four" mean an affirmative answer. Look up "affirmation" in a thesaurus to find other meanings for this word.
2. Who or what groups do you know that might use this code term? (Police, ham radio operators, businesses, ships, and airplane radios.)
3. Help the students invent a code for the alphabet. Write the code on the chalkboard. Then have them each write a coded message. Exchange the papers and have each person decode the message on the paper.

6 CHILDREN'S DAY

Celebrate by:

1. Divide the class into the number of class periods you have per day. Assign each group one of the subject areas. Have each group create a plan for "teaching" the period. Meet with the groups individually and discuss their plans.
2. Have each student make a creative headband identifying their group subject.
3. Have each group wear their headbands, as they implement their ideas and teach the subject at the given period.

6 AMERICAN LIBRARY ASSOCIATION'S FOUNDER'S DAY

Celebrate by:

1. This association was founded in Philadelphia in 1876 for librarians and others interested in libraries. Discuss what it would be like if there were no school or public libraries.
2. The American Library Association awards the Caldecott and Newbery Awards for children's books. Find out for what these awards are given and for whom they were named. Check through the library to find these award books to bring to class. They will have the award seals on the front covers.

8 WORLD'S LARGEST PIZZA
Celebrate by:
1. The world's largest pizza was baked on this date in 1978 in Glens Falls, New York. It was 80 feet in diameter and weighed nine tons. It was cut into 60,318 pieces. Ask students for a way we could make a circle 80 feet in diameter on the playground.
2. Visit a pizza place. Have students take notes on what goes on behind the scenes at a pizza place. Assign students to ask questions the class may have such as; what is the largest pizza you bake; the smallest; how many do you sell in a day or a week; which pizza is the best seller?
3. Use the information in your notes to write a story on the "Hidden Secrets of Making Pizza" or a similar title.
4. Give each student a copy of "Weight-E-Problem" (page 146) to complete.

9 LEIF ERIKSON DAY
Celebrate by:
1. Leif Erikson made a big discovery—what was it and when was it?
2. Give each student a copy of "A Ship's Tale" (page 147) to complete.
3. Leif Erickson's life was told and recorded in stories called sagas. A saga is the name in literature, usually of an adventure, written in Iceland between 1100 and 1300. Saga means "to say" or "to tell." Write a saga about the voyage you took with your friend, Leif Erikson.

11 NATIONAL JOGGING DAY
Celebrate by:
1. Plan a "cross-state" and a "cross-city" jog-a-thon. Have students decide the best way to find the distance (in miles) across your city and state. Figure out how many days it will take you if you jog one mile a day. Decide how far you will jog at school and home (if this is acceptable). Challenge students who are capable, to complete the jog across the city and across your state.
2. Start jogging a little each day, increasing the distance throughout the week. Ask students the best way to find out how many miles it is across the United States. Help them figure out how many days it would take to jog across the United States if they jogged ten miles a day, seven days a week.

12 COLUMBUS DAY
Celebrate by:
1. Observed on this date from 1934–1970. On June 28, 1968, a proclamation was made that it would be celebrated on the second Monday in October, starting in 1971. If Columbus Day were observed as a legal holiday throughout all the states, how would you like to see your family celebrate?
2. After your study of Columbus, have students write down the answers to: what was Columbus' first name; from what country did he sail; what were the names of the King and Queen who sent him on his voyage; when did he land in America; what were the names of his ships?

15 WORLD POETRY DAY

Celebrate by:

1. This day is in celebration of the birthday of the ancient poet, Virgil, who was born in 70 B.C. Have each student bring in his or her favorite poem to read.
2. Read your (teacher) favorite poem to the class. Invite the principal, secretary or custodian to come and read their favorite poems to your class.
3. Invite someone from a local writer's club who writes poetry to come and talk about his or her poetry writing and how he or she submits poetry for publication. Ask a librarian (or check the *Children's Writers and Illustrators Market*, a Writer's Digest Publication) for names of magazines where students can submit poetry.
4. Recite your favorite poem to the class and then challenge them to memorize a short poem.

16 DICTIONARY DAY (WEBSTER'S BIRTHDAY)

Celebrate by:

1. Dictionary Day is also Noah Webster's birthday (1758–1843). He compiled *Webster's Dictionary*, the first American dictionary, which was published in 1806. How long ago was that? The goal of Dictionary Day is to have every person own and use a dictionary. Ask how many students have their own dictionaries. Suggest this might be a good gift to ask for on birthdays or holidays. Find out how many dictionaries are in the classroom and in the school library.
2. Explain how to use the dictionary and some of the information it contains. Give each student a slip of paper with an unfamiliar word on it. Before the end of the day, have them check the meanings of the words and share them with the class. Write the new words on a classroom chart. Review them over the next few days, asking students for the meanings.

18 ALASKA PURCHASED FROM RUSSIA

Celebrate by:

1. Find Alaska and Russia on the map. Give each student a copy of "Alaska! Alaska!" (page 148) to complete.
2. Write a story using, "Way up north in the land of ice and snow" for a story starter.

20 P.T. BARNUM FIRST INTRODUCED HIS CIRCUS

Celebrate by:

1. Phineas Taylor Barnum opened the first circus in America at the Hippodrome in New York City in 1871. He called it "the greatest show on earth." Ask students to share about circuses they have attended. Ask what were their favorite acts.
2. Discuss the similarities and differences between a circus and a carnival; between a circus and a zoo.
3. Read *Circus! Circus!* a poetry book by Lee Bennett Hopkins (Knopf).

21 INCANDESCENT LAMP DEMONSTRATED

Celebrate by:

1. *See:* February 11, Thomas Edison's Birthday. On this date in 1879, Thomas Alva Edison, an American inventor, demonstrated one of his many inventions—the incandescent lamp. What was it? What was used before this invention?
2. The first electric light bulb only burned for 13 1/2 hours. Check the cartons from several different light bulbs to see how long electric light bulbs burn today.
3. Thomas Edison is credited with more then 1,000 inventions. Assign each student to find out about several of his inventions and bring pictures of them to display on the bulletin board.

24 ADMIRAL RICHARD EVELYN BYRD'S BIRTHDAY (1888–1957)

Celebrate by:

1. Admiral Byrd and his dogs, Igloo and Chinook, went on an expedition. Where did they go and what did they discover? Find this place on the map or world globe.
2. Have each student find out two important facts about Antarctica. Add the information to a classroom chart.

24 UNITED NATIONS DAY

Celebrate by:

1. On this date in 1945, the charter was officially signed, marking the founding of the United Nations, but United Nations Day was not proclaimed until 1948. Find out: what is the United Nations Organization; what is its purpose; how does it help people, nations, and governments?
2. UNICEF is an agency of the United Nations. What is UNICEF and what is its purpose?

25 PICASSO'S BIRTHDAY (1881–1973)

Celebrate by:

1. Pablo Picasso was born in Malaga, Spain. Locate this place on a map. His most famous contribution to art was Cubism. He provided clues to his "hidden pictures" type of art. Check with an art teacher or an art history book for pictures of his work to share with students. Study the art works and have students experiment with this technique. Some children's magazines have pages of "hidden pictures" that could be used as an example.
2. Picasso introduced torn pieces of newspaper clippings, bits of debris, and stenciled words into his art pieces. Students can duplicate this art form by pressing similar materials onto a sheet of paper that is first covered with a mixture of paint and liquid glue.
3. Have each student write down three adjectives that describe Picasso's art. Read these to the class.

27 NAVY DAY

Celebrate by:

1. Navy Day has been observed on this date since 1922. Celebrations usually include parades, ship and station open houses and other events. If any students are from a navy family they may know of special events, and they may have family members who would come to speak to your class.
2. Make arrangements to take students aboard a navy ship. Exhibit pictures of navy ships on the bulletin board and invite students to add to the display. Try to find out the different names of the vessels.
3. Compare a ship to a submarine.

27 THEODORE ROOSEVELT'S BIRTHDAY (1859–1919)

Celebrate by:

1. Theodore (Teddy) Roosevelt was a hunter. Find out what the connection is among Teddy Roosevelt, his hunting trips, and teddy bears.
2. Theodore Roosevelt was a true public servant, holding many positions. Have each student find out four different positions he held during his lifetime.

28 NATIONAL PLUSH ANIMAL LOVERS' DAY

Celebrate by:

1. This special day is also celebrated on Teddy Roosevelt's birthday. The day is to honor the friendship, companionship, and support that plush animals provide for millions of adults and children.
2. Have each student write his or her name on a piece of paper and the category of plush animals that he or she predicts is the favorite among the students. Collect the papers. Have each student bring in his or her favorite plush animal, a photograph, or a picture cut from a catalog. Graph the collection and have students compare their predictions to the graph results.
3. Discuss possible fundraisers that your class or school might undertake to raise money to buy plush animals to give to a charity group that collects toys for Christmas.

Last Sunday DAYLIGHT SAVINGS TIME

Celebrate by:

1. At 2 a.m. on this date, we turn our clocks back one hour. Have students find out when daylight savings time started, why it started, and how it affects people in transportation and communication.
2. Set up a debate on whether we should keep or do away with daylight savings time.
3. Write a short story about how you handled daylight savings time in the clock shop you own.

31 HALLOWEEN (ALL HALLOW'S EVE)

Celebrate by:

1. Create a mask, hat, or costume from recycled materials. Share with the class ways your creation can be recycled again.
2. Provide two small pumpkins. Cut one into a Jack-o-Lantern. Have students predict which one will mold first or if they will both start to mold at the same time. Observe daily and record observations in a log. After the cut one starts to develop mold, predict how long it will take the uncut one to develop mold. Use a magnifying glass to examine the mold. Discuss what causes the mold and why the uncut one did not mold as quickly (it may last for months!).

31 JULIETTE LOW'S BIRTHDAY (1860–1927)

See: March 12, Girl Scout Founding Anniversary; 2nd week of March, Girl Scout Week. Juliette Low founded the Girl Scouts of America on March 12, 1912. She was born in Savannah, Georgia.

31 MOUNT RUSHMORE COMPLETED (1941)

Celebrate by:

1. Find out what students know about Mount Rushmore. The memorial is located in the Black Hills, South Dakota (south of Rapid City). Locate it on a map.
2. The monument took fourteen years to complete. Who was the carver of the mountain? Find out how this memorial came into being and more about the man who carved it.
3. The heads of four presidents appear on the 60-foot tall sculpture. Who are these presidents? Locate a picture of the memorial. If students have visited Mount Rushmore, ask them to share any souvenirs they may have.

31 NATIONAL MAGIC DAY

Celebrate by:

1. *See:* 3rd week of October, National Magic Week. Traditionally celebrated on the date of Harry Houdini's death on this date in 1926. Have students find out who Houdini was and what the term magic means.
2. Have students check out books from the library on magic tricks. After reading through the books, have each student select one trick to present to the class. Allow time for practice either at home or at school before your "magic show."
3. Check with a local magic shop, recreation center or library to see if there is someone in your area who does magic shows. Invite him or her to come and perform a few tricks for your class.

31 NEVADA ADMISSION DAY

Celebrate by:

1. Nevada became the 36th state in 1864. Add this information to your United States map (page 13). Color the state lightly with colored pencil or crayon.
2. Write this state opposite its number on the State Admission Order page (page 15).

October, 3rd Week—NATIONAL DENTAL HYGIENE WEEK

MY TOOTH

Place the correct number before the matching part.

_____ Enamel

_____ Crown

_____ Dentin

_____ Root canal

_____ Root

_____ Pulp

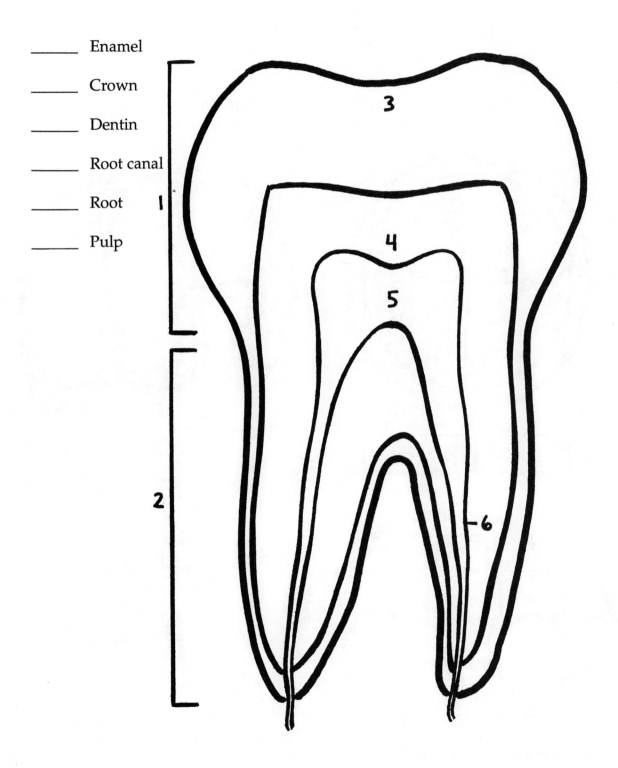

Name _____

October 8—WORLD'S LARGEST PIZZA

WEIGHT-E-PROBLEM

The world's largest pizza weighed 9 tons.
Jumbo, an African elephant, weighed 7 tons.
An American car weighs 1 1/2 tons.
There are 2,000 pounds in a ton.
How many pounds do you weigh?

Figure out how many pounds each of the above weighs.
Write the tons and the pounds under each.

tons   Pounds

tons   Pounds

tons   Pounds

tons   Pounds

Name _____

October 9—A SHIP'S TALE

Write a description of Leif Erickson's ship inside the ship picture.

October 18—ALASKA PURCHASED FROM RUSSIA

ALASKA! ALASKA!

Find Russia and color it green.
Find Canada and color it yellow.
Find the city that is the farthest west and color it brown.
Find the city that is the farthest south and color it blue.
Find the city that is the farthest east and color it red.

November

Flower – Chrysanthemum
Birthstone – Topaz

November is the eleventh month of the year. "Novem" is the Latin word for nine. November was the ninth month in the Roman Calendar. It has 31 days, but originally had only 30 days.

MONTH

AVIATION HISTORY MONTH
Celebrate by:
1. *See:* December 17, Wright Brothers' First Flight. Two brothers, Jacques and Joseph Montgolfier, invented the first balloon to carry people into the air. It was made of paper and cloth. Assign a group to report on the brothers and the first balloon flight.
2. If anyone has been up in a hot air balloon, ask him or her to share the experience. Assign a small group to report on hot air balloons today.
3. Assign groups to report on blimps and airships.

NATIONAL BREAD BAKING MONTH
Celebrate by:
1. Also known as National Family Bread Baking Month. Make bread using a basic recipe. Use frozen unbaked bread loaves to make clover leaf rolls. Pull off small pieces of dough, form the dough into three small balls, and place in cupcake pans. Follow directions for baking.
2. On a class chart, list different kinds of bread such as rye, whole wheat, cracked wheat.
3. Arrange to visit a bakery. Buy a loaf of fresh baked bread (and a jar of jam). Upon returning to the classroom, discuss the visit, read *Bread and Jam for Frances* by Russell Hoban (Scholastic) and then serve bread and jam.
4. Encourage students to plan a "family bread baking day" with their families.

NATIVE AMERICAN INDIAN HERITAGE MONTH
Celebrate by:
1. This special month was proclaimed on October 30, 1991. Many states and tribes have their own local celebrations. Check to find out what is planned in your area.
2. On your state map, locate any Native American tribes and/or reservations (include those in neighboring states).
3. Make copies of the United States map for each student. Locate various tribal reservations or sections where there are large groups of Native Americans, and color in the areas.
4. Invite someone of Native American ancestry to come visit and share the history and arts and crafts of his or her people.
5. Visit a Native American museum. Contact the local National Historical Museum to see if a member could make a school visit.

NATIONAL DRUM MONTH
Celebrate by:
1. Discuss the different kinds of drums, and where we would hear drums being played. Locate pictures, display them on the bulletin board, and learn the names of the drums.
2. Visit the school music department and ask the teacher to give a demonstration on the drums.
3. Play music that includes drums and have students listen for the drums.
4. Make drums from round oatmeal or salt boxes or coffee cans (cover the ends with pieces from an inner tube and lace in place with heavy twine). Beat out rhythms.

WEEK

2nd week NATIONAL CHEMISTRY WEEK
Celebrate by:
1. Chemistry is the study of chemicals and how they react with each other. National Chemistry Week was established to help people recognize how chemistry affects every part of our lives. Select simple chemistry experiments for your students. Some easy and safe experiments can be found in *Chemistry Experiments*, Mary Johnson (Usborne); *Chemistry Experiments for Children*, Virginia Mullin (Dover); *Simple Chemistry*, John Paull (Ladybird Books).
2. Have each student find out one way chemistry contributes to modern life and write a short report.

2nd week NATIONAL SPLIT PEA SOUP WEEK
Celebrate by:
1. Make split pea soup from dried split peas. The recipe can be found on the bag. They can be cooked on a stove, in an electric fry pan, or crock pot.
2. Make a split pea collage.
3. Ask students if they think split peas will sprout on wet cotton, and to give a reason for their answers. Test to find out.

1st full week before Thanksgiving AMERICAN EDUCATION WEEK
Celebrate by:
1. This week was first proclaimed on October 30, 1985. Why do you think it was proclaimed as such?
2. Trace (asking for student input) the pathway of education or teaching. Where does education start (list on a chart)—at home—infant, toddler, prekindergarten, kindergarten, and so on?
3. Have each student write a short essay on why he or she does or does not want to go to college.
4. Have students draw floor plans of your classroom on large sheets of paper. Draw in and label everything they would have in it if they could furnish it anyway they liked in order to make learning more fun.

3rd week NATIONAL CHILDREN'S BOOK WEEK

Celebrate by:

1. Have students, over the week's period, bring in one of their favorite books. Have them report the title, the author, and just enough of a summary to make other students want to read it.
2. Assign each student to check out a book from the school library and read it to his or her family sometime during this week. Remind them to tell their parents this is National Children's Book Week.
3. Arrange to have a children's book author or illustrator visit your class. For names of authors, check with your local children's librarian, or a local writers' group.

3rd week NATIONAL GEOGRAPHY AWARENESS WEEK

Celebrate by:

1. Blow up and give each student a copy of the United States map (or a world map). Have each student glue it to a piece of tagboard. Tell them into how many pieces (the number depends on the ability of the students) to cut the map for a puzzle. Have them mix up the pieces and work the puzzles.
2. Provide envelopes for the puzzle pieces. Number the envelopes and each day pass out a different puzzle to each student to work.
3. Prepare another puzzle, but cut the states apart (cut two or three small states together). Place the pieces in a paper bag. Have each student draw one piece and trace around it on a sheet of paper. Have each identify the state and find out the name of the state flower, bird, and animal. Write the information under the traced state.
4. Place the cut-apart state pieces in a bag. Place in a "center." At free time, students can work with a partner to draw a state from the bag and name it.

4th week LATIN AMERICAN WEEK

Celebrate by:

1. Latin American Week was established to promote an understanding of Latin American countries. Display a large world map. Point out the location of the Latin American countries. Have students go to the world map and point out and name a country. Write the countries on a classroom chart as they are named. Older students can also name and locate the capitals.
2. Write the name of each Latin American country on a separate slip of paper. Place them in a paper bag. Have each student draw a country on which to report.
3. Make a copy of "Latin America Map" (page 158) for each student to use. Make a copy of "Traveling South" (page 159) for each student to complete

4th week NATIONAL BIBLE WEEK

Celebrate by:

1. Ask students to bring in Bibles used in their homes, churches, or synagogues, or a Bible in another language. Have students explain about their Bibles.
2. Compare the similarities and differences.
3. Have students share their favorite Bible verses. Have them share their favorite Bible characters and tell what they like about them.
4. Challenge students to set a goal to read and/or memorize one verse (or more) a week.

4th week NATIONAL FARM-CITY WEEK

Celebrate by:

1. Draw a line down the middle of a classroom chart. Divide it into city kids and country kids. With input from students, list the chores of each. Compare the chores.
2. Read, or tell orally, a version of "The Country Mouse and the City Mouse."
3. Have each student write a modern tale about one mouse who lives in the country and one who lives in the city.

4th Sunday before Christmas START OF ADVENT

Celebrate by:

1. Ask, "What is Advent and why and how is it celebrated?"
2. Talk about the different kinds of possible Advent calendars we could make. Assign students a home project to make an Advent calendar to bring to school. After sharing their calendars, students can take them home.

DAY

1 FIRST WHITE HOUSE FAMILY

Celebrate by:

1. The White House became the official home of the United States president in 1800. Our second president, John Adams, and his wife, Abigail, were the first presidential family to live in the White House. On 3" x 5" cards, write a number for one of our presidents starting with number three. Make a card for each student. Have them find the name of the president and his wife, and write both names on the card (#2, John Adams, Abigail). Older students can add a sentence about the president and about his wife.
2. Children also lived in the White House over the years. Locate one or all of these books to share with the class. *White House Children* by Miriam A. Bourne (Random House); *Amy Carter; Growing Up in the White House* by Alma Gilleo (Child's World); *Growing Up in the White House: The Story of the President's Children* by Seymour Reit (Macmillan).

1st Tuesday ELECTION DAY

Celebrate by:

1. Election Day is always the first Tuesday, after the first Monday in November. National elections are held every four years to elect a president. What is the name of the president elected in the last election? What is the name of the vice president elected in the last election?
2. Invite someone who works at the voting polls to visit your class and answer questions asked by the students.
3. Secure copies of voter's information leaflets at the post office or library for students. Several days before election day, discuss some of the issues and some of the candidates. Make a copy of the ballot for each student to fill out. Assign people to serve in registering, placing ballots in the box, counting ballots, and announcing the results at the end of the class election.

2 NORTH DAKOTA ADMISSION DAY

Celebrate by:

1. North Dakota became the 39th state in 1889. Add this information to your United States map (page 13). Color the state lightly with colored pencil or crayon.
2. Write this state opposite its number on the State Admission Order page (page 15).

2 SOUTH DAKOTA ADMISSION DAY

Celebrate by:

1. South Dakota became the 40th state in 1889. Add this information to your United States map (page 13). Color the state lightly with colored pencil or crayon.
2. Write this state opposite its number on the State Admission Order page (page 15).

3 SANDWICH DAY (JOHN MONTAGUE'S BIRTHDAY 1718–1762)

Celebrate by:

1. The Fourth Earl of Sandwich created the world's first fast-food; he invented the sandwich! One day, being in a hurry to eat, he slapped a piece of meat between two slices of bread. This new creation was called "a sandwich" after the Earl. Have students write the names of their favorite sandwiches on slips of paper. Collect the papers and assign students to sort and count the votes.
2. Provide each student with a piece of wax paper for a work area. Provide plastic picnic knives, bread, butter, and small containers of parsley, celery and carrot sticks, pieces of bell peppers, and bacon bits. Have students spread a bread slice with butter and then use the ingredients provided to make a funny face open sandwich.

6 JAMES NAISMITH'S BIRTHDAY (1861–1939)

Celebrate by:

1. *Quiz:* Ask if anyone knows who James Naismith was. Write the following clues on the chalkboard, one at a time. In 1891, he was asked to come up with a game that could be played indoors; he divided his group into two teams of nine players each. Mr Naismith then hung two peach baskets from the gym balcony. What was this game he invented? (He invented basketball. Basketball became an Olympic sport in 1936.)
2. The ball Mr. Naismith used was a soccer ball. Discuss ways the game has changed since the first basketball game.
3. For younger children, use a safe indoor ball and improvise a basket. Draw a chalk line and let them practice making baskets. For older students, set up a round-robin on a basketball court. Have each student take two shots and pass the ball on to the next person.

7 ELEPHANT BECAME SYMBOL OF THE REPUBLICAN PARTY

Celebrate by:

1. The elephant first appeared in a political cartoon in *Harpers Weekly* magazine in 1874. The Republican party voted to have it be a symbol of their party. Have students find out the symbol for the Democratic party and how it came into being.
2. List some places where we might see these two symbols, such as posters, buttons, and banners.
3. Design a button and a banner for one of the political parties.

8 MONTANA ADMISSION DAY

Celebrate by:

1. Montana became the 41st state in 1889. Add this information to your United States map (page 13). Color the state lightly with colored pencil or crayon.
2. Write this state opposite its number on the State Admission Order page (page 15).

8 X-RAY DISCOVERY DAY (1895)

Celebrate by:

1. Dr. Wilhelm Conrad Roentgen of Germany is given credit for discovering X-rays. Ask how many students have had X-rays (teeth, broken bones), and if anyone knows for what the "X" in X-ray stands (x is a scientific symbol that stands for the unknown). Ask students to tell about their experiences with X-rays.
2. Check with a parent or doctor for old X-rays of different parts of the skeletal system for students to examine.
3. Ask the school nurse to explain how X-ray machines work.

10 MARINE CORPS' BIRTHDAY

Celebrate by:

1. The United States Marine Corps was established on this day in 1775. It was originally a part of the navy but became a separate branch of the service on July 11, 1789.
2. Look at pictures of navy and marine uniforms and discuss the similarities and differences.
3. Ask if students have family members who are or have been in the marines. Invite a marine or former marine to come and talk to your students and wear or bring a uniform, pictures, and medals.

11 VETERAN'S DAY (ARMISTICE DAY)

Celebrate by:

1. This day was first celebrated in 1919, and has been declared a holiday by Presidential proclamation since 1926. It was formerly called Armistice Day, but was changed on June 28, 1968 to Veteran's Day. Find out why and where the first holiday was held and why the name of the day was changed.
2. A moment of silence is observed on this day at 11 a.m., the eleventh hour of the eleventh month on the eleventh day. Hold a moment of silence in your classroom at this time and ask students to think of someone they know who has served in the armed forces.
3. Make a class card, or individual cards, thanking veterans for serving our country. Mail it to a veteran's hospital or veteran's organization.

11 WASHINGTON ADMISSION DAY

Celebrate by:

1. Washington became the 42nd state in 1889. Add this information to your United States map (page 13). Color the state lightly with colored pencil or crayon.
2. Write this state opposite its number on the State Admission Order page (page 15).

13 PEANUT BUTTER INVENTED

Celebrate by:

1. *See:* March, National Peanut Month. Make peanut butter in an old fashioned, food grinder, and in an electric blender. (Use Spanish peanuts with skins, and grind or blend until it can be spread, no oil or salt is needed.)
2. Compare the two results. Spread both kinds of peanut butter on crackers for a taste test.

16 OKLAHOMA ADMISSION DAY

Celebrate by:

1. Oklahoma became the 46th state in 1907. Add this information to your United States map (page 13). Color the state lightly with colored pencil or crayon.
2. Write this state opposite its number on the State Admission Order page (page 15).

17 HOMEMADE BREAD DAY

Celebrate by:

1. *See:* November, National Bread Making Month. Make special bread today, such as raisin, cinnamon or French bread.
2. Discuss the role yeast plays in bread dough, and why it is important to use only the amount called for in the recipe.
3. Have each student write a story about the day he or she put too much yeast in the bread dough.

17 NATIONAL YOUNG READER'S DAY

Celebrate by:

1. *See:* 3rd week in November, National Children's Book Week. Make a list of all the books students have read since school started this fall.
2. Make copies of "My Read! Read! Read! Chart" (page 160) for each student.
3. Have each student read a book to a non-reader. Share the experiences.

18 GREAT AMERICAN SMOKE-OUT

Celebrate by:

1. *See:* May 31, United Nations No-Tobacco Day. Make a poster with a message for Great American Smoke-Out Day. Ask permission to display the posters around the school.
2. Have students encourage a friend, family member, or neighbor to join the Great American Smoke-Out.

18 MICKEY MOUSE'S BIRTHDAY

Celebrate by:

1. *See:* June 9, Donald Duck's Birthday. On this day in 1928, Mickey Mouse, first appeared on screen as "Steamboat Willie." It was the first animated talking picture.
2. Use round objects found in the classroom and have students trace around a large one for Mickey's head, and around a smaller one for the ears, and then add the facial features. If desired, cut out and attach to a headband.
3. Give students a copy of "Mickey Mouse's Puppets" (page 161) to color and cut out. After making the puppets, have students work in small groups to present a puppet show.

19 GETTYSBURG ADDRESS

Celebrate by:

1. The anniversary of the Gettysburg Address is celebrated with a brief memorial service at 10 a.m., at the Soldier's National Monument in Gettysburg, Pennsylvania, at the National Cemetery. Read the Gettysburg Address to the class.
2. The Gettysburg Address was only a two minute speech. Find out: Who wrote it, when, where, and why it was written? Where is the original located?
3. Divide the class into three groups and have each group read sections of the Address in unison.
4. Challenge older students to memorize the Gettysburg Address.

Sunday before Thanksgiving MOTHER GOOSE PARADE

Celebrate by:

1. *See:* May 5, Mother Goose Day. This parade, the only one of its kind, takes place in El Cajon, California. It began as "a gift to the children" and consists of many floats representing a variety of Mother Goose characters. Bring in a collection of Mother Goose Rhyme books. Have students take turns reading a rhyme.
2. Have each student write his or her favorite Mother Goose rhyme on a slip of paper. Collect the papers and sort to find the top three favorites.
3. Have each student illustrate his or her favorite rhyme. Number the illustrations (but no names). Display the art work. Have students write the numbers on sheets of paper and the name of the rhyme they think is illustrated in each picture.

3rd Thursday THANKSGIVING

Celebrate by:

1. Have students divide a sheet of paper down the middle. On one side, write how the first Thanksgiving was celebrated. On the other side, write how their families spent, or will spend, this Thanksgiving.
2. Research the changes that have taken place in the date for celebrating Thanksgiving. Make a time line to show the changes. Start with the first celebration on December 4, 1619 and end with the present day.

21 NORTH CAROLINA ADMISSION DAY

Celebrate by:

1. North Carolina became the 12th state in 1789. Add this information to your United States map (page 13). Color the state lightly with colored pencil or crayon.
2. Write this state opposite its number on the State Admission Order page (page 15).

21 WORLD HELLO DAY

Celebrate by:

1. Say, "Happy Hello Day," to five people (other than your classmates) sometime today. At the end of the day, have students share the reactions of some of the people to whom they wished a Happy Hello Day.
2. Say, "hello," to the first student, and go around the room having everyone give a different greeting such as hi, howdy, how-you-doing. Write each greeting on the chalkboard.
3. Have each student find a greeting in a different language to share with the class, such as aloha, güten tag, bonjour, and give the country of the language.

30 SAMUEL LANGHORNE CLEMENS' BIRTHDAY (1835–1910)

Celebrate by:

1. Ask if anyone can tell you the pen name of this man (Mark Twain). He was born in Florida, Missouri, on this date in 1835. He owned many animals and had four cats named Belzebub (prince of the devils), Blatherskit (nonsense talk), Apollinaris (Greek God of Sunlight), and Buffalo Bill. Why do you think he chose these names, and how do you think each cat behaved based on its name? If you were given a cat today, what name would you give it and why?

2. Mark Twain traveled widely and gathered material for the many books he wrote. Read aloud parts from *Adventures of Huckleberry Finn*, *Adventures of Tom Sawyer*, and *The Prince and the Pauper*.

3. Mark Twain said, "I came in with Halley's Comet and expect to go out with it." What did he mean by this?

LATIN AMERICA MAP

Study the map. On a separate sheet of paper do the following: Make a list of all the Latin American countries. Put the countries in alphabetical order.

Name _____

November, 4th Week—LATIN AMERICAN WEEK

TRAVELING SOUTH

Use your Latin American Map to find the answers.

Which country is the largest? _____

Which country is the smallest? _____

Which country has a canal cut through it? _____

Which country extends the farthest east? _____

Which country is the farthest north? _____

Which county extends the farthest south? _____

How many countries are there in South America? _____

How many Central American countries are there? _____

Name _____

November 17—NATIONAL YOUNG READER'S DAY

MY READ! READ! READ! CHART

Starting today, keep a list of the books you read.

Date	Title	Author	Main Character

November 18—MICKEY MOUSE'S BIRTHDAY

MICKEY MOUSE'S PUPPETS

Color and cut out the puppets.
Overlap the band around your finger and tape in place.

December

Flowers – Holly, narcissus, poinsettia
Birthstones – Turquoise, zircon

December is the twelfth and last month of the year. "Decem" is the Latin word for ten. In the Ancient Roman calendar, December had twenty-nine days and was the tenth month.

Ask students if they know of other words that start with "deca" such as decade and decapod, and discuss the relationship of the words to "ten."

MONTH

BINGO'S BIRTHDAY MONTH
Celebrate by:
1. Play a game of bingo. Discuss how the game is set up and how it is played.
2. Have small groups create and design a bingo game for math, spelling, opposites, or other subject areas.
3. Ask parent helpers to make cards using the students' ideas for a bingo game.
4. Let a few students at a time check out the bingo sets to take home to play with family members or friends.
5. Arrange with the teacher of a younger group of students to have your class (or a group) explain their bingo game and play it (or regular bingo) with the younger students.

UNIVERSAL HUMAN RIGHTS' MONTH
Celebrate by:
1. Ask students for the meaning of the term, "human rights."
2. Have each student list five rights he or she is entitled to as a citizen of the United States.
3. Have students list five responsibilities they have toward others as citizens of the United States.
4. Ask if citizens in all countries enjoy the same rights that we do. Can they think of other countries that do not enjoy these rights?
5. On a class chart, list what rights students feel all individuals should be entitled to no matter where in the world one lives.

WEEK

10–16 HUMAN RIGHTS WEEK
See: December, Universal Human Rights' Month; December 15, Bill of Rights Day.

2nd week NATIONAL METRIC WEEK
    See: December 23, Metric Conversion Act Anniversary.

2nd week TELL SOMEONE THEY ARE DOING A GOOD JOB WEEK
Celebrate by:
1. Have students, each day during the week, tell at least one person that he or she is doing a good job. Have each student keep a log of the day and the time he or she did this kindness and write two sentences about the experience.
2. Think of people outside your classroom who you think are doing a good job. Send a "doing a good job" note or card, sing a song or recite a poem, or give flowers from your yard to at least one person during this week.

16–24 POSADAS
Celebrate by:
1. This is a nine day celebration throughout Mexico and many areas in the United States. Ask if anyone knows what Posadas means. The word translates as shelter. Ask someone familiar with this celebration to come and explain it to the students (or find information in a book) and help the students plan a Posadas presentation.
2. Find out how to make, or ask a parent of Mexican descent to come and help students make, a large papier-maché piñata for the class. Older students can make smaller individual piñatas.

Last two weeks AUDUBON CHRISTMAS BIRD COUNT
Celebrate by:
1. *See:* April 26, John Audubon. This event has been annually celebrated since 1900. Ask students what they think the celebration is about, and why it is celebrated. (It is a census of winter bird life of the continent.) See what information students can find out about this day. Contact an Audubon Society member for additional information. Also check newspapers for articles on this event.
2. Have students keep a log of the birds they see during this two week period. Have each student describe each bird, when and where he or she saw it, and draw a picture of each bird.
3. Provide encyclopedias and bird books for students to identify the names of the birds they saw. Take a count of the birds seen by all the students.
4. Ask students: if you were a bird, which one would you wish to be? Write a paragraph telling why you chose this bird.

DAY

3 ILLINOIS ADMISSION DAY
Celebrate by:
1. Illinois became the 21st state in 1818. Add this information to your United States map (page 13). Color the state lightly with colored pencil or crayon.
2. Write this state opposite its number on the Admission Order page (page 15).

7 DELAWARE ADMISSION DAY
Celebrate by:
1. Delaware became the 1st state in 1787. Add this information to your United States map (page 13). Color the state lightly with colored pencil or crayon.
2. Write this state opposite its number on the Admission Order page (page 15).

7 PEARL HARBOR (1941)
Celebrate by:
1. Ask if anyone knows what happened on December 7, 1941. Explain that this was the date of the Japanese aircraft attack on Pearl Harbor, Hawaii. Locate Pearl Harbor and Japan on the map.
2. Explain that on this date, our President signed a declaration of war against Japan—our entry into World War II. Have students find out who was president at the time. He said these famous words, "December 7, 1941 is a date that will live in infamy." Ask students what they think this meant. Have someone look up "infamy" in the dictionary and read the definition to the class.
3. Find out if anyone has been to Hawaii and visited Pearl Harbor and the National Monument. Ask them to tell about their visit.

9 EMMETT KELLY'S BIRTHDAY
Celebrate by:
1. *See:* 1st week in August, National Clown Week. Emmett Kelly, a sad-faced hobo clown who wandered around the circus in his baggy pants and hat, was born on this day in 1898. He was one of our most famous clowns. See what else students can find out about this clown.
2. Provide paper plates and decorating materials for students to make a clown mask. They can cut large eye holes, punch holes on both sides of the plates and attach long cut rubber bands.
3. Have each student draw a picture of a clown he or she would like to be if he or she had a job in the circus.
4. Provide ONLY construction paper, scissors, and glue for students to make a cut-and-paste clown.

10 MISSISSIPPI ADMISSION DAY
Celebrate by:
1. Mississippi became the 20th state in 1817. Add this information to your United States map (page 13). Color the state lightly with colored pencil or crayon.
2. Write this state opposite its number on the State Admission Order page (page 15).

11 INDIANA ADMISSION DAY
Celebrate by:
1. Indiana became the 19th state in 1816. Add this information to your United States map (page 13). Color the state lightly with colored pencil or crayon.
2. Write this state opposite its number on the State Admission Order page (page 15).

12 FIRST TRANSATLANTIC WIRELESS SIGNAL (1901)
Celebrate by:
1. Guglielmo Marconi (1874 –1937), an Italian inventor born on April 25, 1874, developed the first radio. He sent the first transatlantic wireless signal on this date in 1901. Make a list of uses for radios outside the home—police, firefighters, pilots, taxi cabs. Find out more about Marconi.
2. Demonstrate how a clock radio works.
3. On a classroom chart, list the kinds of information we might hear on a radio. Ask why a radio, with fresh batteries, is important to have on hand in case of an emergency, and what some of these emergencies might be.
4. Ask parents for old radios that don't work. Provide screwdrivers and small pliers for the students to take apart, examine, and reassemble the radios.
5. Discuss how sound is imitated in radio scripts. As a class, write a radio skit with sound effects and do a short radio broadcast.

12 PENNSYLVANIA ADMISSION DAY
Celebrate by:
1. Pennsylvania became the 2nd state in 1787. Add this information to your United States map (page 13). Color the state lightly with colored pencil or crayon.
2. Write this state opposite its number on the State Admission Order page (page 15).

12 POINSETTIA DAY
Celebrate by:
1. Dr. Joel Roberts Poinsett (1799–1851) introduced this colorful Central American plant into the United States. He brought back a plant when he returned from a visit there, and the plant was then named for Mr. Poinsett. Find Central America on the map. Display a fresh poinsettia plant and point out the unusual flowers. Provide magnifying glasses for students to examine the plant. The tiny yellow flowers are surrounded by the colored (generally red) bracts. These red bracts are not the leaves; the green parts are the leaves.
2. Have students note the different colors of poinsettias to be found during this month (white, pink, salmon, variegated).
3. In some tropical countries, a poinsettia plant may grow as high as ten feet. Measure the height of your plant. How much taller is a ten foot tropical poinsettia than your plant?
4. Using thick red, green and yellow finger paint, paint a picture of a poinsettia plant.

14 ALABAMA ADMISSION DAY
Celebrate by:
1. Alabama became the 22nd state in 1819. Add this information to your United States map (page 13). Color the state lightly with colored pencil or crayon.
2. Write this state opposite its number on the State Admission Order page (page 15).

14 SOUTH POLE DISCOVERED

Celebrate by:

1. *See:* April 6, North Pole Discovered. The South Pole was located by Roald Amundsen (1872–1928) on this day in 1911. He took with him on his trip fifty sled dogs. What is the South Pole? Locate it on a world globe or map.

2. Assign small groups to find out: what kind of transportation did he and his group use; what was his original destination and what made him change his mind; how many people started out in Amundsen's party and how many reached the South Pole; what country's flag was the first to fly over the South Pole; what kind of plant and animal life can be found there today; who are the people that can be found there today and what are they doing at the South Pole?

15 ALEXANDRE GUSTAVE EIFFEL'S BIRTHDAY (1832–1923)

Celebrate by:

1. *See:* March 31, Eiffel Tower Anniversary. This Frenchman designed the Eiffel Tower and also helped design the Statue of Liberty. Where was the Eiffel Tower built, and why was it built?

2. Assign each student to find the height and weight of both the Eiffel Tower and the Statue of Liberty, and then make a vertical graph to show the comparison.

15 BILL OF RIGHTS' DAY

Celebrate by:

1. This day is celebrated as the anniversary of the acceptance of the Bill of Rights as Amendments to the Constitution in 1791. Ask if anyone knows what the Bill of Rights is (the first ten Amendments to the Constitution).

2. Divide the class into ten groups. Give each group a number and have them find the name of that particular right and write it on a classroom chart, that you have numbered from one to ten.

3. Have each group read, in unison, when their number is called.

4. Have each student write down which right from the Bill of Rights he or she thinks is the most important one and why.

16 BOSTON TEA PARTY (1773)

Celebrate by:

1. Ask students if they have ever been to a tea party. Then ask if they know which tea party was the largest one in history. Bring in a large clear glass bowl. Have a student fill it with water. Have another student slowly pour in a quarter cup of tea leaves. Say nothing for a few seconds, then say simply that this is what happened at the world's largest tea party, but at that tea party, tea was not emptied into a bowl. It was dumped into the sea. This tea party took place in Boston and was known as the Boston Tea Party. Ask students what they know about this event.

2. Have each student find out three things about the Boston Tea Party and present the facts to the class.

17 WRIGHT BROTHERS' FIRST POWERED FLIGHT

Celebrate by:

1. *See:* April 16, Wilbur Wright's Birthday; August 19, Orville Wright's Birthday. This day in 1903 marked their "heavier than air" airplane flight. Discuss what this term means. Find out where this event took place and then locate the place on a map.
2. Contact a hobby or a model airplane group and see if someone would come and give a demonstration of powered model planes.
3. Check with students to see if they have ever made a model airplane, or if someone in their families has. Ask those students if they can answer questions about model airplanes that the other students might have.

18 NEW JERSEY ADMISSION

Celebrate by:

1. New Jersey became the 3rd state in 1787. Add this information to your United States map (page 13). Color the state lightly with colored pencil or crayon.
2. Write this state opposite its number on the State Admission Order page (page 15).

18 NUTCRACKER BALLET FIRST PERFORMED (1892)

Celebrate by:

1. The Nutcracker Ballet was first performed in Russia on this day in 1892. Ask how many students have seen the Nutcracker Ballet on stage or TV. Check the local newspapers or a cultural arts center to see if there is a performance scheduled near you.
2. Ask if anyone takes ballet. If so, ask him or her to share his or her shoes and dance costume and tell about the dance. Check with a dancer in the community who may be able to come and give a ballet demonstration.
3. Read *A Very Young Dancer*, by Jill Krementz (Knopf) or check with the librarian for another story about the ballet.

19 CHRISTMAS GREETINGS FROM SPACE

Celebrate by:

1. On this date in 1958 at 3:15 p.m. (E.S.T.), the United States Earth satellite, ATLAS, transmitted the first radio voice broadcast from space. Assign students to find out what this 58-word recorded Christmas message was ("To all mankind, America's wish for peace on earth and good will toward men everywhere.") and whose voice it was (President Dwight Eisenhower).
2. If you could send a 58-word (or less) Christmas message from space today, write down the message you would send.

21 or 22 WINTER BEGINS

Celebrate by:

1. This day marks the beginning of winter for the United States. What season is starting in Australia? in England? in Germany?
2. Find out: What determines the change in seasons? What is the winter solstice?
3. Have each student write a paragraph describing the first day of winter where you live.

21 NATIONAL FLASHLIGHT DAY

Celebrate by:

1. The first day of winter has the shortest amount of daylight hours. Which day this year is the "longest night of the year"? If a flashlight were your only means of light, which night of this year would you use your flashlight the most?
2. Bring in different sizes and kinds of flashlights. Darken the classroom and have students work in small groups, each using a flashlight, and have a "light show," chasing each others' beams, and crossing and circling the rays of light.
3. Show students how to take a flashlight apart, how the batteries and bulb work to produce a light, and how to reassemble the flashlight. Let students take turns taking apart and reassembling a flashlight.

23 METRIC CONVERSION ACT

Celebrate by:

1. The Metric Conversion Act, on this day in 1975, called for a voluntary change over to the metric system. On a classroom chart, list any signs of change-over observed in your community or state, such as speed limit signs and gasoline pump measuring systems.
2. Give each student a copy of "Metric Time Line" (page 171) to complete.

25 CLARA HARLOWE BARTON'S BIRTHDAY (1821–1912)

Celebrate by:

1. *See:* May 8, World Red Cross Day. Clara Barton founded the Red Cross in America on May 21, 1881. How long has there been a Red Cross in the United States? Read a biography on Clara Barton to the class.
2. List some of the disasters (fires, floods, earthquakes) where the Red Cross helps and some of the things the Red Cross probably does to help. List the organizations or groups in your community that help people in time of disaster or personal need.

25 CHRISTMAS DAY

Celebrate by:

1. This day is celebrated in Christian countries throughout the world as the birthday of Jesus Christ. How many Christmas days have there been? How many Christmas days have you celebrated?
2. Discuss the word "tradition." Have students write down the traditions held by their families during this month. Have students take turns reading their family tradition list.
3. Bring in a live tree in a pot. Have students decorate the tree using ornaments made from recycled materials. When school closes for vacation, find out about placing it in the local library, a bank, or a store. Make sure students are responsible for removing the tree after the holidays. Donate the tree to a park.
4. Have a "Charlie Brown Christmas tree" by placing a dead tree branch in a pot of wet sand, and having the students make decorations from recycled materials. Before vacation, turn it into a "bird tree," by placing it outdoors and hanging berries, pieces of bread, and seeds on its branches.

26 BOXING DAY

Celebrate by:

1. Boxing day is a special day in Canada, Australia, and England (as well as some other countries). Ask for input as to why students think this day is special in those countries. Boxing Day is the first workday (usually the day after Christmas) after Christmas when postal carriers and other public servants receive Christmas "gift boxes." Have students make small thank you notes for the school postal carrier, place them in a gift box and arrange to meet the carrier and present the box.

2. Have students write essays on why they think the United States should or should not have a "Boxing Day."

26–January 3rd KWANZAA

Celebrate by:

1. Find out if you have students who can tell the class about this special day, or ask someone from the community to visit and explain the celebration and show the celebration dress, photographs, and share the seven principles. Kwanzaa is the Swahili word for "first fruits." Kwanzaa, a black family observance in recognition of the traditional African harvest festival, has been officially observed in our country since 1966.

2. Celebrate the end of the seven day festival with a "harvest feast" (karamu) or one traditional dish.

28 POOR RICHARD'S ALMANAC ANNIVERSARY (1732)

Celebrate by:

1. *See:* July, Read an Almanac Month. On this date, the *Pennsylvania Gazette* carried the first newspaper ad for the first almanac by Richard Sanders. Who was Richard Sanders? (Benjamin Franklin) Find out how many pages were in his almanac and how many pages are in one of the almanacs, today.

2. After having students look through almanacs, have them each write a newspaper ad for one of today's almanacs.

29 TEXAS ADMISSION DAY

Celebrate by:

1. Texas became the 28th state in 1845. Add this information to your United States map (page 13). Color the state lightly with colored pencil or crayon.

2. Write this state opposite its number on the State Admission Order page (page 15).

31 NEW YEAR'S EVE

Celebrate by:

1. Discuss how families celebrate New Year's Eve. Also discuss the danger of fireworks and firearms for use in celebrating. Discuss things we could use for noise-makers for our family celebrations.

2. Ask the name of the traditional New Year's Eve song. The song, "Auld Lang Syne," is a Scottish poem and the words are Gaelic for "long ago." Recite it first to your students as a poem, and then have them join you in singing it.

3. Robert Burns is given credit as the author of the poem. Have students do research on this author. Read other poems he wrote.

25th day of the Hebrew month HANUKKAH (CHANUKAH)

Celebrate by:

1. Hanukkah is an eight-day Jewish holiday beginning on the 25th day of Kisleve (the Hebrew calendar). The holiday celebrates the rededication of the Temple of Jerusalem. Locate a Jewish parent or friend who can come in and explain how the holiday is celebrated.

2. Ask someone who is knowledgeable on Jewish celebrations to come and help the students make a Jewish food dish, sing or play appropriate music, explain the menorah, and help students make a dreidel.

METRIC TIME LINE

1821	John Quincy Adams proposed the conversion to the metric system.
1886	Congress legalized the use of the metric system.
1890	Attempts were made by Congress to change U.S. measurements to metric.
1957	The United States Army and Marine Corps adopted the metric system for its weapons and equipment.
1968–1971	Congress recommended that the United States convert to the metric system.
1975	The United States Congress passed the Metric Conversion Act.

Use this information to make a time line.